Mexicans and Mexican Americans in Michigan

Rudolph Valier Alvarado
and
Sonya Yvette Alvarado

Michigan State University Press

East Lansing

∞ The paper used in this publication meets the minimum requirements
of ANSI/NISO Z39.48-1992 (R 1997) (Permanence of Paper)

Michigan State University Press
East Lansing, Michigan 48823-5245

Printed and bound in the United States of America

10 09 08 07 06 05 04 03 1 2 3 4 5 6 7 8 9 10

LIBRARY OF CONGRESS CATALOGING-IN-PUBLICATION DATA
Alvarado, Rudolph.
Mexicans and Mexican Americans in Michigan / Rudolph Valier Alvarado
and Sonya Yvette Alvarado.
p. cm. — (Discovering the peoples of Michigan)
Includes bibliographical references and index.
ISBN 0-87013-666-6 (pbk. : alk. paper)
1. Mexican Americans—Michigan—History. 2. Mexican Americans—Michigan—Social
conditions. 3. Mexicans—Michigan—History. 4. Mexicans—Michigan—Social conditions.
5. Immigrants—Michigan—History. 6. Michigan—Ethnic relations. 7. Michigan—Social
conditions. I. Alvarado, Sonya. II. Title. III. Series.
F575.M5 .A45 2003
977.4'00468073—dc21
2002153202

Discovering the Peoples of Michigan. The editors wish
to thank the Kellogg Foundation for their generous support.

Cover design by Ariana Grabec-Dingman
Book design by SharpDes!gns, Inc., Lansing, Michigan

Folklorico dancers, courtesy of Julian Samora Research Institute,
Michigan State University

Visit Michigan State University Press on the World Wide Web at:
www.msupress.msu.edu

To our fathers:
Dennis Casarez and G. N. Robertson,
who taught us to respect hard work
and learning.

SERIES ACKNOWLEDGMENTS

Discovering the Peoples of Michigan is a series of publications that resulted from the cooperation and effort of many individuals. The people recognized here are not a complete representation, for the list of contributors is too numerous to mention. However, credit must be given to Jeffrey Bonevich, who worked tirelessly with me on contacting people as well as researching and organizing material.

The initial idea for this project came from Mary Erwin, but I must thank Fred Bohm, director of the Michigan State University Press, for seeing the need for this project, for giving it his strong support, and for making publication possible. Also, the tireless efforts of Keith Widder and Elizabeth Demers, senior editors at Michigan State University Press, were vital in bringing DPOM to fruition.

Otto Feinstein and Germaine Strobel of the Michigan Ethnic Heritage Studies Center patiently and willingly provided names for contributors and constantly gave this project their tireless support. Yvonne Lockwood of the Michigan State University Museum has also suggested and advised contributors.

Many of the maps in the series were prepared by Gregory Anderson at the Geographical Information Center (GIS) at Western Michigan University under the directorship of David Dickason. Additional maps have been contributed by Ellen White.

Other authors and organizations provided comments on other aspects of the work. There are many people that were interviewed by the various authors who will remain anonymous. However, they have enabled the story of their group to be told. Unfortunately, their names are not available, but we are grateful for their cooperation.

Most of all, this work is a tribute to the writers who patiently gave their time to write and share their research findings. Their contributions are noted and appreciated. To them goes most of the gratitude.

ARTHUR W. HELWEG, *Series Co-editor*

Contents

Preface

A few years ago, my family and I sold our house in Texas, packed our belongings into a U-Haul truck, and moved to Michigan, after I accepted a position at Henry Ford Museum and Greenfield Village. My brother-in-law drove the truck, while my wife and I shared the responsibility of driving the family car. In the car with us were our two children and my daughter's cat. We drove north, taking the same route my mother and her family had traveled as migrant farm workers decades earlier.

My family and I knew no one in Michigan. My mother had distant relatives living in Kalamazoo and a sister in Chicago. However, because I was born and raised in Texas, I did not know any of them well. Years before, these relatives had settled in *el norte* (the north) after a season of harvesting, due to the economic opportunities the north offered. In his first year in Chicago, my aunt's husband left the fields for the railroad yards. Their family grew. They soon purchased a home, and with time came to own a whole city block.

My own family has likewise continued to grow. My wife and I now have three additional children born in Michigan; we are buying our home; and we have made a number of friends. My wife teaches at Eastern Michigan University. In the summer of 1999 I left my position with Henry Ford Museum and Greenfield Village to accept a position with the Spirit of Ford, a short-lived interactive science center owned by Ford Motor Company. After leaving the Spirit of Ford, I found it difficult to choose what to do next. I could have returned to teaching, or sought a job as a program developer for a museum, but if I had made the decision to do that it would have meant the real possibility of uprooting my family yet again.

After consulting with my wife and children, it was decided that we would stay in Michigan and take our chances. So far, the move has paid off. My wife is doing exceptionally well in her position, and my children are doing well in school. My wife and I have written a book published by the University of Michigan Press, and I have a book published by Alpha Press/Pearson Education. I have also taught a class titled "The History of Latinos in the United States: From Origin to the Present" at the University of Michigan. When I am not writing or teaching, I have managed to find steady work as a carpenter with my good friend Dan Taylor.

I begin this work in this way not because I want the reader to hire me to write a book or to build a house, but to impress on the reader that my story is not essentially different from that of the Mexicans and Mexican Americans who settled in Michigan before me or those who came and will continue to come to Michigan after me. My story might not include a stop at the sugar beet fields, or at a Ford factory, but like those before me, I, too, came in search of a better life for myself and for my family. I have adapted to the world around me as necessary for the security and survival of my family, and have not been ashamed to do what it takes to make sure that my family and I can stay in the state we choose to call home.

When I was a boy my mother spoke to me of the sugar beet fields of Michigan. She also spoke of autumn trees, of cold mornings, and of long days. Her stories led me to become an ardent fan of Michigan football (of which Michigan team, I will never tell). When the opportunity arose and I was able to watch my favorite Michigan football team on the television, my stepfather, Dennis, always laughed at me when I'd tell him that one day I'd be standing in the team's stadium. He used to chuckle, saying there was no way a Mexican boy from *tejas* (Texas) could ever make it that far north, except to find himself in a field picking pickles; certainly never in a football field for some fancy university. My stepfather passed away long before I made it to Michigan, yet somehow when I stood in that stadium and whispered hello to him, I knew he heard me. So it is that I dedicate this book to him, not only because he placed before me the challenge of proving him wrong, but because he taught me to respect learning, and how to use a hammer and nails.

In closing, Sonya and I would like to acknowledge the contributions made by the following individuals and organizations to the success of this book: David Conklin, Elizabeth Demers, Margaret Garry, Arthur Helweg, Marta Lagos, Lowell G. McManus, Maria Elena Rodriguez, Dolores Sanchez, and the staffs of the Bentley Historical Library, the Detroit Public Library, the *Detroit Free Press*, the *Detroit News*, the Detroit Tigers, the Walter Reuther Library of Labor and Urban Affairs, the Burton Historical Collections, the Michigan State Library and Archives, and the Michigan State University Museum.

Special thanks are also extended to Dr. Israel Cuéllar and Danny Layne of the Julian Samora Research Institute for providing a host of photographs used in this book. We are most grateful for the willingness of Romie Minor and Melissa Haddock of Henry Ford Museum and Greenfield Village Research Library to go above and beyond the call of duty in obtaining the photograph regarding Henry Ford while their department was in the process of moving into their new facility. We also want to offer a special word of thanks to Laurie Kay Sommers for her guidance in obtaining the use of the photograph concerning the Circulo Mutualista Mexicano and the Cruz Azul.

Finally, we want to acknowledge the work of the following eminent scholars and historians, whose research and publications we turned to in writing portions of this book: Malvina Hauk Abonyi, Rodolfo Acuña, Marietta Lynn Baba, George T. Edson, David W. Hartman, Carey McWilliams, Eduard Adam Skendzel, Dennis Nodín Valdés, Julian Samora, and Zaragosa Vargas.

Introduction

The history of Mexicans and Mexican Americans in Michigan is one rooted in economic opportunity. It is the story of families who, like other immigrants from all over the world, came to the state in search of a better life. However, the story of Mexicans and Mexican Americans in Michigan differs from those of their immigrant counterparts in that most of them did not arrive and stay, but arrived, worked, and then returned home to the southwestern United States or Mexico until the following season, when they returned to work in the fields of Michigan once again. It was not until the decade starting in 1910 that Mexicans and Mexican Americans began to settle in Michigan. As might be expected, these early Mexican and Mexican American pioneers were small in number. However, by the 1920s the number of Mexicans and Mexican Americans settling in Michigan began to grow from one year to the next.

The history detailed here by no means represents the complete story of Mexicans and Mexican Americans in Michigan. Instead, it focuses on settlement trends and the growth of the population. It also examines the cultural and social impact the state had, and continues to have, on Mexicans and Mexican Americans, and vice-versa. The terms Mexican and Mexican American are meant to represent those

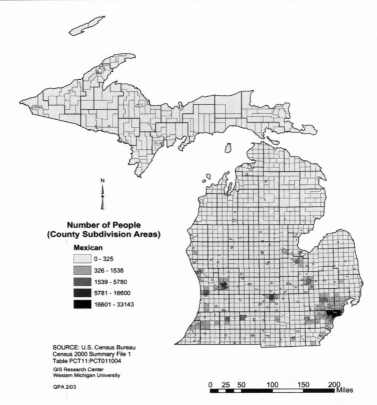

Distribution of Michigan's population claiming Mexican ancestry (2000).

individuals that claim the country of Mexico as their point of origin. The use of these terms is by no means meant to neglect those who prefer to be referred to by another name, such as Latino, Mestizo, Hispanic, Chicano, or American. The terms Mexican and Mexican American are used solely for the purpose of avoiding confusion. As a matter of fact, the terms are often used side by side, and alone, in order to clarify the group being referred to in the text. Similarly, the terms Hispanic, Spanish-speaking, and Spanish-speaker are used as generalized terms representing Mexicans, Mexican Americans, Latinos, Puerto Ricans, and so on. Again, this is done to avoid confusion, and is by no means meant to demean the contributions made by any of these groups.

It must also be clarified that when references are made to United States census records, this is done with the understanding that these numbers are not always exact because of a variety of issues unique to Mexican immigrants. For example, from the time of the earliest census records to the most recent, Mexicans have often not been included in the census count because they have entered the country illegally, and thus have not answered the door when the census takers have come calling.

Finally, this work is undertaken with the hope that it will spur others to add to the study and research of Mexicans and Mexican Americans in Michigan and throughout the United States. Archival collections housed by a variety of universities and research centers throughout the state and the country contain a wealth of history just waiting to be tapped into and written about.

This, then, is the story of Mexicans and Mexican Americans in Michigan. Enjoy!

The Making of the Mexican and Mexican American People

The origin of the Mexican people dates back to around 10,000 B.C., when Asiatic tribes crossed the Iberian Peninsula and eventually made their way down into the Western Hemisphere. The members of these tribes were nomadic hunters who followed the herds of buffalo, mammoths, mastodons, and other large animals that existed at the time. With the coming of a drier environment about 7500 B.C., the herds that had once sustained life could not find enough vegetation to support themselves; this eventually lead to their downfall. To survive, tribes hunted small animals and picked berries and wild seeds.

By 5000 B.C., tribes residing in the Puebla region of Mexico had learned how to grow plants for food. Chief among these was corn. However, they also raised avocados, beans, peppers, squashes, and tomatoes. For meat they hunted small game and raised turkeys and dogs. These developments allowed tribes to form permanent farming settlements in the southern highlands and forests, and on the rich and fertile south-central Valley of Mexico, especially along Lake Texcoco. To sustain the growing population, farmers developed irrigation techniques that allowed them to produce even more food. With the growth of villages people developed specialized skills in a number of areas.

This new class of people included pottery makers, priests, and weavers, to name but a few.

By 500 B.C., villagers had erected pyramids with flat tops, on which a temple was placed. Select villages, such as Cuicuilco, near present-day Mexico City, became centers of religious activity. People came from all walks of life and from great distances to worship at these religious centers. In time these villages grew in enormous proportions and could be found scattered throughout present-day Mexico.

The first of the indigenous people to make strides toward civilization in Mexico were the Olmec Indians of the southern Gulf Coast. The civilization was to last from 1200 B.C. to 100 B.C. During this span of time, the Olmecs developed a counting system and a calendar, and carved beautiful stone statues. The Olmecs, however, were but a shadow of great civilizations to come. The Classic Period of Mexico, which lasted from A.D. 300 to A.D. 900, ushered in a number of cultures that flourished for a period of time and then mysteriously faded away, or grew small in number or influence. Among these was that of the Mayans, a group that developed extensive libraries, paved roads, originated the concept of zero, and developed hieroglyphic writing. There were also the warring Toltecs, who established an empire in the 900s with its capital at Tula, north of present-day Mexico City. After invading the Yucatán Peninsula, the Toltecs rebuilt the Mayan religious center of Chichén Itza and became an influential presence in the central and southern regions. Among their strongest influences were the worship of the feathered-serpent god Quetzalcoatl and the practice of human sacrifice during religious ceremonies.

The last of the great Mexican cultures was that of the Aztecs. The Aztec kingdom extended from the Gulf Coast to the Pacific Ocean and from the Isthumus of Tehuantepec north to the Pánuco River. Their capital was established in 1325 and was named Tenochtitlán. It was built on an island in Lake Texcoco, the site of present-day Mexico City. Rich with gold and silver, the Aztec empire grew to a population of approximately 100,000 by the time the Spanish arrived in 1519.

With the appearance of Spanish conquerors, the history of the region now called Mexico and its people were altered for all time. The Spanish not only established colonies in present-day Mexico, the

Caribbean islands, and the southeastern United States, they also founded settlements in what became the southwestern United States. With the establishment of these settlements came a social order in which full-blooded Spaniards born in Spain held the highest rank, while indigenous people and Mestizos, individuals born from the mixture of Spanish blood with that of the indigenous population, held the lowest. Referred to as *peninsulares*, full-blooded Spaniards born in Spain held an even higher social standing than full-blooded Spaniards born in the New World, who were referred to as Creoles. To *peninsulares* went top government positions, which allowed them to control commerce and the distribution of the wealth accumulated from business dealings.

With time the people living under the subjugation of the Spanish elite became disheartened. Revolutions erupted, led by men like Father Miguel Hidalgo y Costilla and Father José María Morelos y Pavón, but they were quickly dispelled. When liberal forces gained control of Spain in 1820, Ferdinand VII accepted a constitution curtailing his power. Fearing that the new political atmosphere in Spain would mean social reforms, conservative leaders in New Spain, who were led by Vicente Guerrero, joined forces in an attempt to overthrow Spanish rule. To safeguard their position of power and their holdings on the other side of the Atlantic, the liberals of Spain sent Agustín de Iturbide to crush the rebellion. However, when Iturbide arrived in New Spain, he joined forces with Guerrero, and together they declared Mexico's independence in February 1821. This led to a number of battles between Mexican and Spanish forces that ended with the defeat of Spanish forces before the end of the year.

Free from Spanish rule, the people living in the newly established country of Mexico could not agree upon a form of government. Conservatives favored a member of Spain's royal family to serve as ruler, while liberals wanted a republic. Still a third group called for the installment of Iturbide as emperor. The matter, however, became moot after Iturbide declared himself emperor in 1822. Because of his poor leadership, Iturbide's reign came to an end in 1823, when the Mexican army, led by General Antonio López de Santa Anna, ousted him from power, and Mexico was declared a republic. A constitution was written, and two houses of government were established. Elected as the country's first president was Guadalupe Victoria, a former disciple of Fathers Hidalgo and Morelos.

Over the decades that followed, the people of Mexico struggled to maintain a stable government. At one point Santa Anna supported the formation of a republic, and he was even elected as president of the country in 1832. However, after a series of events in which Congress passed a number of liberal measures, Santa Anna took control of the country by declaring himself dictator in 1834.

In the years prior to relinquishing control of New Spain, the Spanish government had allowed Americans to settle in present-day Texas. This move was designed to counter an interest shown in the territory by a number of foreign powers, namely the French. By the time Santa Anna came to power in Mexico there were a number of Americans living in Texas. With Santa Anna's rise to power, Americans residing in Texas became concerned with the potential effect this would have on their lives and their property. After a series of failed attempts at negotiating an agreement by which their ownership of property would be recognized by the Mexican government, the American settlers revolted in 1835. This led to the defeat of the American forces at the famous Battle of the Alamo at San Antonio in 1836. However, before the end of the year Texas forces regrouped and crushed Santa Anna at the Battle of San Jacinto. During the battle, Santa Anna was captured. To save himself, he negotiated and signed a treaty recognizing Texan independence. The Republic of Texas was to include parts of present-day Colorado, Kansas, New Mexico, Oklahoma, and Wyoming. The agreement led to the political downfall of Santa Anna, at least for the time being. The Mexican government, however, refused to recognize the treaty, claiming that Santa Anna had no right to enter into an agreement on behalf of the Mexican people.

The matter came to a head in 1845, when Texas was admitted into the United States. This led to a number of skirmishes along the Texas-Mexico border. To safeguard American citizens, American forces were sent into the area in April 1846. When Mexican forces attacked them, America declared war. Led by General Zachary Taylor, the American army came to occupy much of Mexico. Taylor became a national figure and was elected president in 1848. In 1847, General Winfield Scott captured Mexico City after the Battle of Chapultepec, a battle in which a number of young military students chose to leap over a cliff to their deaths rather than surrender.

Soundly defeated, the Mexican government signed the Treaty of Guadalupe Hidalgo in February 1848. Under the terms of the agreement, Mexico gave up its claim to present-day California, Nevada, and Utah, as well as parts of Arizona, Colorado, New Mexico, and Wyoming. Texas was also recognized as a part of the United States, down to the Rio Grande. Among other considerations, for their part, Americans paid Mexico fifteen million dollars and granted Mexicans living in territories now belonging to the United States full rights as citizens of the United States.

This meant that the more than eighty thousand Mexican Americans living in these regions could count on the United States to safeguard their civil and political rights, could worship freely, and could know that their property rights would be recognized and protected. However, the rights guaranteed them under the Treaty of Guadalupe Hidalgo were not readily upheld. Mexican Americans lost lands that had been in their families for generations, and when gold was discovered in California and the Gold Rush of 1849 sent thousands of Americans west in search of their fortune, Mexican Americans were displaced from their lands and were driven out of mining camps through intimidation and by the passage of laws that prohibited them from being financially able to hunt for gold. Even so, some Mexican Americans managed to keep control of their land, and to make headway into the new social and political order in which they found themselves. Men like Miguel Antonio Otero of Arizona, Mariano Vallejo of California, Diego Archuleta of New Mexico, and Santos Benavides of Texas prospered and became leaders in their own right, and when America's Civil War erupted in 1860, over 10,000 Mexican Americans took part , an astonishing number when it is noted that the U.S. Census of 1860 showed that there were only 26,477 Mexican Americans living in the United States.

With the end of the Civil War, Mexican Americans not only faced situations similar to those they had encountered before the start of the Civil War, but also found themselves in the precarious position of being in demand as a source of cheap labor, spurred on by the growth and expansion of the railroad, mining, and farming industries. In the railroad industry, Mexicans and Mexican Americans were needed to complete and maintain railroad lines after the depression of the mid-1870s led Congress to pass the Chinese exclusion acts in 1882, 1892, and 1902, designed to ease competition from Chinese labor. Further adding to America's need for Mexican and Mexican American labor was the Gentleman's Agreement with Japan in 1907 that excluded working-class Asians. In the mining industry, Mexicans and Mexican Americans were needed to work existing mines and the large number of copper and silver mines that were coming into being, because they could now be worked at a profit with the establishment of a railroad network in the Southwest. In the field of farming, cheap labor was needed to work the more than 1,446,000 acres that were being cultivated by 1900.

Responding to this demand for laborers were Mexicans and Mexican Americans who were drawn by the promise of good pay and the opportunities and security such money would bring to their families. So overwhelming was the Mexican response to the need for laborers in the United States that the American census of 1900 showed that there were 103,393 Mexicans in the United States, a significant increase over the 77,853 Mexicans found to be residing in the United States at the time of the 1890 census.

Time and the onrush of Mexicans who entered the United States did nothing to curtail the need for laborers. From 1900 to 1910, U.S. Census records show that the Mexican population more than doubled, to 221,915. With the start of World War I in 1914, the demand for agricultural and industrial workers soared even higher, due to a number of variables. These variables included the fact that America was the chief supplier to the Allies, the labor shortage brought on after young Anglo-Americans joined the armed forces, and the reduction of European immigrants into the United States after the start of the war. Even though American industrial concerns had made some effort to recruit Mexicans and Mexican Americans in the past, their efforts to entice Mexicans and Mexican Americans to work for them increased dramatically following the start of World War I. In towns and cities like Mexico City, El Paso, Laredo, Ft. Worth, and San Antonio, Mexicans and Mexican

Americans were recruited and hired to work in the various branches of California's agriculture, the beet fields of Colorado and Michigan, the cotton fields of Texas, the copper mines of Arizona and New Mexico, and the meat-packing houses of Chicago. They were also employed by the automotive plants of Detroit, the iron foundries of Pennsylvania and New York, the Appalachian coal mines, and on railroad gangs all over the United States.[1] So effective were recruitment efforts that according to the census of 1920, the number of Mexicans in the United States had more than doubled again since 1910, to a total of 486,418.

Mexicans and Mexican Americans took advantage of the employment opportunities being offered to them to better their lives and those of their families. In Mexico, where the population of the country had soared to over six million by the turn of the century, people were eager to land a job in the United States. Adding to their willingness to make the trek north was the lack of land available to them on which to farm, and the political turmoil that seemed to always rock the country. Most important, however, was the money that they could earn in the United States. It was not long before Mexican colonies could be found in cities like St. Paul, Milwaukee, Chicago, Gary, Toledo, and Pittsburgh. There was also a sizable Mexican colony in the industrial city of Detroit.

Early Mexican and Mexican American Pioneers in Michigan

When compared to most of the ethnic groups residing in Michigan, Mexicans and Mexican Americans are relative newcomers to the Wolverine State. According to the U.S. Census of 1900, there were 56 Mexicans living in Michigan. By 1910 there were 82, and while the census of 1920 found that there were 1,268 Mexicans in Michigan, historians estimate that the number was really well over 4,000 in Detroit alone. The reason for the growth of the Mexican and Mexican American population of Michigan during the decade from 1910 to 1920 has been traced to four primary factors. The first was the start of World War I, which created a labor shortage. The second was the announcement by Henry Ford in 1914 of the five-dollar day, and the third was the arrival in Detroit of Mexican railroad employees from a variety of states to do the work once reserved for men who were now serving as soldiers in Europe. The final reason for the growth of the Mexican and Mexican American population of Michigan was the economic boom that followed World War I. During this boom, the Southern and Eastern European immigrants rose up the economic ladder, which meant they moved out of jobs that were then relegated to Mexicans and Mexican Americans. The majority of Mexicans who settled in Michigan at this time hailed from the Mexican states of Chihuahua, Durango, Zacatecas,

Jalisco, Guanajuato, and Michoacan, while Mexican Americans hailed from the southwestern United States, primarily Texas.

The largest number of these early arrivals resided in Detroit. However, by the time the U.S. Census of 1920 was taken, Mexicans could also be found in the towns of Saginaw (98), Flint (82), Pontiac (46), Port Huron (39), Battle Creek (25), and Grand Rapids (19). According to Catholic Church records and Ford Motor Company employment records, three-fourths of these individuals were single men, or solos, ranging in age from twenty to twenty-nine years of age, while only two percent were age forty or over.[2] Most of those that were married sent for their families once they were settled and could afford the cost of transporting them. Employed primarily as *traqueros* (railroad workers) by companies such as Michigan Central, some of these early pioneers soon found themselves in line outside of Henry Ford's Highland Park plant in the hope of landing a five-dollar-a-day job. Some did, while others found work in steel mills, or other factories, such as Briggs or Saginaw Grey Iron.

The greatest percentage of early Mexican and Mexican American pioneers who settled in Michigan, however, were employed by the sugar beet industry, which eventually paid for the transportation of tens of thousands of Mexicans and Mexican Americans into the state. Companies such as Michigan Sugar, Columbia Sugar, Isabella Sugar, and Continental Sugar recruited these people in Texas cities such as El Paso and San Antonio and in the central states of Mexico. The first trainload of these farm workers arrived in Michigan in the spring of 1915. Adding to the early growth of the Mexican and Mexican American population of Michigan were the migrant farm workers who paid for their own transportation to Michigan, and who decided to leave the fields in search of work in Detroit, Saginaw, Winn, Oil City, or Sheperd. Still others remained in rural areas, where they formed *colonias* (colonies) with names like El Pozo (The Well), El Hoyo (The Hole), and Cuatro Esquinas (Four Corners).[3]

The United States Census of 1920 showed that there were 1,268 Mexicans living in Michigan. Of this number, the report showed that over seven hundred lived in the City of Detroit. Today it is the belief of a number of historians that the actual number of Mexicans and

Mexican Americans living in Detroit by 1920 was over four thousand. In explaining the undercount, historians cite a number of factors. First, they believe that the undercount is based on the fact that Mexican people of the time were a transitory group. Second, a number of Mexicans were not counted because they did not open the door when census takers came knocking, in fear that they would be deported to Mexico. Of course, some of those individuals had a reason to worry, having entered illegally into the United States. Finally, historians feel that a number of single Mexican and Mexican American men were not counted because they did not keep a permanent home in Michigan, or if they kept one, they did not keep it for very long.

Adding credence to historians' belief that there were more than four thousand Mexicans and Mexican Americans living in Detroit by 1920 are a number of newspaper articles published at the time in which reporters cited the same estimate. For example, in his piece titled, "A Little Bit of Old Mexico Right Here in Detroit," which was published in the *Detroit Sunday News* on 5 September 1920, James L. Devlin reported that there were an estimated four thousand Mexicans living in the "Mexican quarter" of Detroit.

Regardless of the discrepancy over the number of Mexicans and Mexican Americans residing in Michigan by 1920, historians agree that on their arrival following the close of World War I, a large number of these residents lived on Third Avenue near Plum Street, and between Grand River Avenue and Abbott Street, along Third, Fourth, and Fifth Avenues. Some Mexicans and Mexican Americans, especially single men, also resided in Highland Park, near Ford Motor Company's Highland Park plant, where they were employed.

After their arrival in Detroit, the experiences faced by Mexicans and Mexican Americans differed from one person to the next. For some, work was easy to come by because they were well connected in Mexico. This allowed them to bring letters of recommendation with them in order to secure work at places like the Ford Motor Company. For others, work was hard to find, for a number of reasons. Some could not speak English, or did not have enough money left over after paying for their journey north to stay in the city for the length of time required to find a job. Others found that jobs were scarce due to production slowdowns or discriminatory practices. To make ends meet, these men turned to working in the sugar beet fields, or took menial jobs wherever they could be found. Some even returned home to Mexico, or the Southwest, while others sought work in other towns and cities of the Midwest.

By the end of the 1920s, the Mexicans and Mexican Americans of Detroit that had weathered the early storm of securing employment and finding a place to live were well on their way to establishing themselves as yet another ethnic group that called the city home. In many ways, they came to emulate the various ethnic groups that had come before them. They founded mutual aid and social societies designed to offer assistance to those in need, as well as to promote and preserve the Mexican culture. For example, Las Casas de Asistencias (The Homes of Assistance) existed solely to provide single men with a hot meal, for which a small amount was sometimes paid, or at least offered in gratitude. These organizations were almost always named after the region in Mexico from which the owner of the home hailed. There was La Michoacana, La Oaxaquena, Ocatlan, San Angel, and so on.[4] Founded in 1920 to promote and preserve Mexico's heritage, as well as to unite the Mexican and Mexican American people, were the Mexican Catholic Society and the Latin-American Club. The Mexican Catholic Society sponsored a number of social events to raise money for building a Mexican Catholic Church. The Latin-American Club was founded by employees of Ford Motor Company, who came from various parts of Latin America, as a way to learn English and the company's business practices before returning home to work for Ford Motor Company branches located in Latin America. The primary function of this group was to provide social and cultural activities to Latin American employees. From this group would emerge a social group composed entirely of Mexicans, called Centro Espanol (Spanish Club). Founded in 1923, this group would be open to all Mexicans and Mexican Americans, not only Latin American autoworkers employed by Ford Motor Company.

In celebration of their culture and heritage, by 1920 the Mexican and Mexican American people residing in Detroit had further established themselves as yet another piece of the rich fabric of Detroit's ethnic society by celebrating El Diez y Seis de Septiembre (The Sixteenth

The Ford Sociological Department

In the 1920s, aside from having trouble securing employment, some Mexicans and Mexican Americans were taken aback by the cost of living in the city of Detroit. When they had been told of the riches that awaited them in the north, they were not told that the higher cost of living would cut into the extra money in their paycheck.

Even so, most Mexicans and Mexican Americans were able to find work. At the Ford Motor Company, as well as at a few other factories, lessons in writing and speaking English were provided for employees free of charge. Ford Motor Company even established the Ford Sociological Department, a department charged with sending representatives to employees' homes, in order to teach them about clean and healthy living and to provide guidance to these employees in a number of additional areas, including how to raise a child, how to save money, how to communicate with one's spouse, and so on. While some historians and sociologists have emphasized the negative aspects of this Ford endeavor, the Mexicans and Mexican Americans of the time saw it as beneficial because they felt it taught them how to become better American citizens.

of September), the day in which Mexico gained its independence from Spain. The Mexicans and Mexican Americans of Detroit hosted a second celebration on 11 December, observing the Feast of Our Lady of Guadalupe. Well over eight thousand Mexicans and Mexican Americans, as well as a number of people from a variety of other ethnic backgrounds, attended the event. In commemoration of this first religious observation by the Mexicans and Mexican Americans of Detroit, a painting of La Virgen de Guadalupe (The Virgin of Guadalupe) was presented to the city fathers.[5]

By 1920, the early Mexican and Mexican American community of Detroit, which was made up almost exclusively of Roman Catholics, worshipped in a double room in Old St. Mary's School under the guidance of Father Jose Alanis, a thirty-five-year-old priest from Mexico. However, Mexicans and Mexican Americans also attended services at the Holy Family Catholic Church on Hastings and East Fort. Of his congregation Father Alanis stated, "My countrymen will prove among the most useful aliens drawn to Detroit in recent years. They came . . . with the expectations of becoming useful citizens. . . . I am confident that we can . . . teach them a sympathetic understanding of the laws and liberties of this Republic."[6]

In the fall of 1920, the Mexican and Mexican American leaders of Detroit announced that in the coming year their community would host a number of events in order to further share its culture with Detroiters. In publicizing plans for the coming event, James Devlin of the *Detroit News* announced the creation of a Mexican troupe of entertainers consisting of singers, dancers, and actors. He wrote that these talented people were found living in the "Mexican quarter of the city." He credited the formation of the troupe to Father Jose Alanis. Devlin went on to write that since its creation the day-to-day operation of the troupe had been turned over to the Mexican Society of Detroit, a social group whose aim was the preservation of the Mexican culture, as well as the creation of a Mexican Catholic church.

When describing the Mexican and Mexican American people living in Detroit at this time, Devlin wrote that he found them to be "progressive Mexicans, pauperized by revolutions, who had fled Mexico to seek opportunity in the northland. Many arrived in Detroit incredibly poor, yet possessing a buoyant hope of finding opportunities here. When they obtained employment, they were happy, because employment here as common laborers was highly preferable to the existence they had lived in their revolution-torn country."[7]

Threatening to put an end to these celebrations and to the growing Mexican and Mexican American population of Detroit was the economic recession that started in the spring of 1920 and lasted into the next year. Rooted in the overproduction of automobiles in most automotive factories except Ford Motor Company, and the loss of military contracts after World War I, the recession meant that Mexicans and Mexican Americans suddenly found themselves playing the role of scapegoat for the economic woes that had taken hold of Michigan, as well as the entire Midwest. "Real" Americans, like some Anglo-American veterans of World War I, blamed Mexicans and Mexican Americans for their inability to find work. Adding to the growing friction between Anglo-Americans and the Mexican and Mexican American people was an influx of thousands of Mexican and Mexican American sugar beet workers into Detroit in the spring of 1920. This occurred after the sugar beet companies of Michigan found that it would not be to their best interest to proceed with a spring planting, or to provide housing for the Mexican and Mexican American sugar beet workers who suddenly found themselves out of a job.

In Detroit, where over eighty percent of the automotive industry's workforce was unemployed, city fathers were faced with a growing dilemma. The cost of providing social assistance for those out of work was rising dramatically. In all of 1920, the cost of providing assistance to needy families was $305,300. In one year this number had jumped to $1,958,300. There was no way that the City of Detroit could continue to support such a figure, and there was no way that the U.S. government could continue to support similar costs across the country. A way of minimizing the number of families and individuals receiving aid from the city, and from the American government, had to be found.

One of the measures implemented was particularly harsh: sweeps were made through neighborhoods and factories, in order to round up and deport Mexicans and Mexican Americans who could not prove legal residency in the United States. It is interesting to point out that in a number of cases sweeps of factories were made before, or on the day when Mexican and Mexican American workers were to receive their paychecks.

A second, less intimidating initiative was also undertaken: voluntary repatriation. Under this program, any Mexican wishing to return to Mexico could do so on a train, free of charge. Paying for much of this expense was the Society of St. Vincent de Paul, a group that raised more than $10,000 for this cause. Supporting their effort was the Mexican Consulate's office, the second such office established in the United States by the Mexican government. Through this office three branches were established in Michigan for the sole purpose of repatriating Mexicans. From November 1920 to February 1921, the repatriation program in Detroit would be responsible for the loss of an estimated 2,500 of the over 4,000 Mexican and Mexican American people who had once called Detroit home. Treatment received by the Mexican people of

Detroit, as well as those living throughout the United States at this time, would serve as a model for what would be done about the Mexican "problem" during the Great Depression, and it gave notice to Mexicans of a fact that holds true even to this day: When the economy of the United States is thriving and there is a need for a cost-effective and reliable labor force, they are welcomed with open arms, but when the situation is reversed they are often the first to lose their jobs, they are denied the privilege of entering the United States in search of employment, or they are deported back to Mexico.

By 1922, the nation's economy was on the rebound. In the Midwest, Mexicans and Mexican Americans once again found work in the fields and in the railroad and steel industries. In Michigan, they found work with sugar beet companies and with automotive and industrial plants located throughout the state. While the Mexicans and Mexican Americans who made their living working off the land returned to Mexico or to the southwestern United States once seasonal work was finished, Mexicans and Mexican Americans entering the Michigan industrial and automotive job market at this time had considerable experience and became permanent residents. Most came from Chicago, Indiana, Ohio, Pennsylvania, and New York, where they had worked in steel mills and foundries. Some also came from Colorado, or Monterrey, Mexico, where they had worked in steel mills. Still others returned to the state hoping to land a job in the automotive industry; the same industry in which they had been employed prior to leaving the state during the rough economic times of 1921.

The most prestigious of all work that a Mexican or Mexican American could secure in Michigan at the time was a job with Ford Motor Company. In Mexico, and throughout the Southwest, Henry Ford's Model T was well known, as was the reputation of the man himself. Among the Mexican and Mexican American population, Henry Ford was known as a fair employer who gave a man a job despite his ethnic background. He paid top wages for a hard day's work, and on occasion men who worked for him spoke to their friends of Henry Ford walking among them, and of times that he stopped and talked with them, or had his photograph taken with them. Accolades were also paid to Henry Ford for providing a school in which men could learn how to speak and

Henry Ford with Mexican and Mexican-American employees outside Highland Park plant in 1919. For Michigan's early Spanish-speaking population a job with Ford Motor Company was considered quite an accomplishment. From the collections of Henry Ford Museum & Greenfield Village.

write English, as well as advance their knowledge and skills regarding automobiles.

Aside from Ford Motor Company, Mexican and Mexican Americans also began working for Buick Motor, who in 1922 hired them for the first time. So receptive were Mexicans and Mexican Americans to the opportunity that four years later there were five hundred Mexicans working in the Buick Motors plant in Flint, Michigan. The 1920s also saw approximately 1,500 Mexicans employed by General Motors and its subsidiaries in Saginaw, Flint, and Pontiac, and hundreds of Mexicans and Mexican Americans could also be found on the payroll of Chevrolet Motors in Flint. Twenty-five were employed in the Oakland Motors plant, and the Wilson Foundry and Machine Company employed two hundred in the making of engine blocks for Wills-Knight Motors. By 1926, Dodge Motors employed three hundred Mexicans in its Hamtramck plant. Twenty of these men were gang bosses, or assistant managers. Limited numbers of

Mexican and Mexican American automotive workers could also be found at Fisher Body, Studebaker, Packard, Maxwell, and Cadillac. In Detroit, Briggs Manufacturing also employed Mexicans and Mexican Americans, and by 1928, of the 5,000 to 6,000 men at the plant, over seven percent were Mexicans and Mexican Americans.[8]

With the growth of the Mexican and Mexican American population of Detroit and the opening of Ford's River Rouge plant, by the mid-1920s Mexican and Mexican American settlements began to emerge in the Michigan-Junction area of Southwest Detroit and in the Old Irish area nicknamed Corktown near the Michigan Central Depot and the Most Holy Trinity Church.

With the formation of these settlements, Mexican and Mexican American businesses catering to the population emerged in a number of areas. From 1918, when there were only two Mexican businesses in operation, both of which were barbershops run out of the owners' homes, to 1924–25, Mexican and Mexican American businesses grew to include eight storefront barbershops, seven restaurants, six grocery stores, a bakery, a boardinghouse, a tailor and dressmaker's shop, a shoe repair shop, and a trucking firm. While the number of Mexican and Mexican American businesses fluctuated over the years, and businesses such as auto repair shops, jewelry stores, pool halls, notary publics, and even doctors' and lawyers' offices opened and closed, by 1928 the list of Mexican and Mexican American businesses in Detroit included eight barbershops, two restaurants, eleven grocery stores, five billiard halls, six boardinghouses, a dry goods store, a bakery, three shoe repair shops, two auto repair shops, a jewelry store, and a lawyer's office. Also included in this list were printing shops, booksellers, cigar makers, a laundry, a beauty salon, and even a business that provided music lessons.[9]

The first newspaper serving the Mexican and Mexican American people, *El Eco de la Patria* (The Echo of the Mother Country), was published during the early history of the Mexican and Mexican American colony. However, by 1921 the publication had fallen silent. A newspaper that served the Mexican and Mexican American community exclusively did not surface again until 1928, with the weekly publication of *El Camello*. A year later, a second newspaper serving the Mexican and

Women in the Job Market

To offset the expenses of moving north, to support themselves and their children, or to supplement their husbands' incomes, Mexican and Mexican American women entered the job market in 1922 in far greater numbers than ever before. Jobs available to them could be found in both the private and the public sectors. Some were employed as domestic help, while others, surprisingly enough, found work in factories and in professional positions. In the area of domestic help, they were employed as janitors, laundresses, cooks, and cleaning ladies. In factories, they held positions as inspectors, packers, markers, sorters, box washers, candy dippers, glasscutters, and solderers. They also served as punch press, drill, lathe, and sewing machine operators. In professional positions, Mexican and Mexican American women were employed in clerical and sales jobs; typical positions held included work as clerks, typists, secretaries, stenographers, bookkeepers, translators, milliners, and saleswomen. Aside from these positions, Mexican and Mexican American women also worked as elevator operators, store cashiers, office messengers, dressmakers, seamstresses, cigar makers, hairdressers, and nurses, and in food service.*

*Vargas, Proletarians of the North, 136; from City of Detroit and Wayne County marriage affidavits for 1918 through 1929 and R. L Polk's Detroit City Directory (Detroit: R. L. Polk Company, 1918–29).

Mexican American people came into being, called *La Gaceta Mexicana* (The Mexican Gazette). This publication was operated by a liberal Mexican named Luis G. Gasca. In that same year, Gasca also founded *Prensa Libre* (the Free Press), which was known for its anti-Catholic news stories. To counter the contents of *Prensa Libre*, in 1930 Simón Muñoz, an early Mexican pioneer to Michigan and an Apostolic Catholic layman, started *La Chispa* (The Spark), which was published biweekly over the next five years. The newspaper contained articles praising the Catholic Church, as well as stories concerning the Mexican and Mexican American community. It also criticized stories in the *Prensa Libre* that were socialist and communistic in nature.

In the area of social and civic responsibility, Mexicans and Mexican

Americans established a number of organizations. In 1922, the Circulo Mutualista Mexicano (Mexican Mutual Aid Circle) was founded in the St. Mary's Catholic Church with the purpose of providing care for Mexicans and Mexican Americans who were sick or homeless. They also sent money to Mexico to help Mexicans in need of assistance. To raise funds, the 150 members of the organization not only paid dues but also raised money by sponsoring, among other events, Saturday night dances that became extremely popular. Also counted among newly established social and civic organizations was La Sociedad de Damas Catholicas (The Society of Catholic Women), La Sociedad de San Jose (The Society of San Jose), and La Cruz Azul Mexicana (The Mexican Blue Cross).

Aside from these mutual aid societies, Mexicans and Mexican Americans further established organizations to promote and preserve the Mexican culture and heritage. Counted among these groups was the Centro Cultura (the Culture Center), founded by upper-middle-class Mexicans and Mexican Americans, an organization where the rich Mexican culture was showcased. There was also El Comite Patriotico Mexicano (the Mexican Patriotic Committee), an organization still active to this day, which organized festivities celebrating Mexican holidays, such as El Cinco de Mayo (The Fifth of May), a day commemorating the defeat of the French in Mexico in the 1860s. This organization also planned and carried out the Feast of Our Lady of Guadalupe and El Diez y Seis de Septiembre, a celebration that came to represent "the most important social event of the year for the Mexican community."[10] Representatives of organizations that existed to promote the Mexican culture and heritage were the Obreros Unidos Mexicanos (Unified Mexican Workers), which promoted the interests of industrial workers; El Club Artístico Femenino (The Ladies Artistic Club), a girls dance group; and the Mexican Catholic Players, a theatre troupe.

In praising the achievements of the estimated seven to eight thousand Mexicans and Mexican Americans residing in Detroit, Charles D. Cameron wrote in the *Detroit Saturday Night* that, "The Mexican colony of Detroit is the best-organized national group we have among us. . . . In every place where a hundred or more Mexicans reside, one will find a "Mexican honorary commission," or Comision Honorifica Mexicana.

Members of Círculo Mutualista Mexicano and Cruz Azul in 1925. Both were lead-
ing Mexican and Mexican American societies in Detroit. This photograph is one
of a few remaining that capture members of the early Mexican and Mexican
American social organizations. Courtesy Michigan Traditional Arts Program.

This commission is in touch with the nearest consular office, so that any member of that community can obtain any consular service."[11]

The formation of these organizations, and others like them, as well as the praises being heaped on the Mexican and Mexican American people gave proof that the Mexican and Mexican American population was becoming firmly established in the city of Detroit. Nothing, however, better served to give notice of this permanence than the founding of the Mexican Catholic church, Our Lady of Guadalupe, on 27 October 1923. Located on Kirby and Roosevelt Streets, the church building was 75' by 25', with a 16' by 16' wing. The Mexican congregation, which at the time numbered 160 families, purchased the land on which it was built for approximately $11,000. Construction on the church building was started on 1 September, and was completed by 27 October. Mass was offered once a day from Monday to Saturday, and three times on Sunday.

Of the church's effect on his congregation that first year, Father Alanís wrote to the bishop of Detroit, "The moral influence of the new church on the Spanish-speaking people of the city, especially on the

Mexican people, is incalculable. Each Sunday the church is filled to overflowing, and the financial recovery of the church is secure. Moreover, a great number of souls will receive important spiritual help through its agency."[12] Led by the charismatic Mexican priest, Father Alanis, in its first three years of existence the church struggled to increase its membership. The difficulty was a result of the church being built some two to three miles away from the core of what was quickly becoming the heart of Detroit's Mexican and Mexican American community. Despite this disadvantage, however, the church's membership grew. According to the annual reports submitted by the church to the bishop of Detroit, by 1927 the number of families attending the church had grown to 500, and by 1928 this number had risen to 520. However, with the onset of the Great Depression, the number of members in the church decreased dramatically, to just 100 in 1929, following the trend in the Mexican and Mexican American population of Detroit as a whole, which decreased from 9,739 in 1930 to 3,694 by 1940.

The Great Depression and Repatriation

With the onset of the Great Depression in 1929, and in the years that followed, a large percentage of the Mexicans and Mexican Americans in Michigan found themselves jobless. In 1929 the sugar beet industry transported its final trainload of Mexican and Mexican American workers, totaling 709 individuals, into the state.[13] At Ford Motor Company's River Rouge plant, 928 Mexicans had been hired for the production of Ford's newly unveiled and extremely popular Model A, but by the next year that number was down to 185. By the end of 1930 all of these workers were without jobs.[14] The effects on the city of Detroit's social programs, as well as on those of the United States as a whole, were similar to those experienced during the economic recession of 1921. To help ease the rising cost of providing for those Mexicans and Mexican Americans in need, repatriation programs were reintroduced in towns throughout Michigan, and across the country.

In Detroit the program was strictly voluntary in nature, though strongly promoted by social workers, as well as employees for the Detroit Department of Public Welfare, the city police, and the U.S. Department of Labor and Immigration. The Mexican consulate in Detroit issued repatriation certificates to one thousand families in 1930, and in 1931, four hundred Mexicans paid their own fare to return to Mexico. The "final cleaning up" of Mexicans and Mexican Americans wishing to return home came in November 1932, when five thousand families and single men were deported.[15]

Though repatriation efforts were well underway by the time the great Mexican muralist, Diego Rivera, arrived in Detroit on 22 April 1932 to paint his now famous mural for the Detroit Institute of the Arts, he was to play a major role in influencing Detroit's Mexican population to return to Mexico. He took this initiative on his own after witnessing conditions in which some Mexicans and Mexican Americans were living. As he toured the city, Rivera saw Mexicans and Mexican Americans living in boxcar camps, in dilapidated one-room apartments, and in tent villages, or standing in bread lines a block long. He met with mothers who, after being abandoned by their husbands, were struggling to feed, clothe, and shelter their children. He was also aware of the Ford Hunger March that had taken place in March 1932, in which three Ford Motor Company employees had been killed after Dearborn police opened fire on three thousand Ford Motor Company employees.

To convince the Mexican and Mexican American people to return to their "homeland," Rivera delivered speeches in which he espoused socialist and communist ideas. He also helped to found and provided financial support for La Sociedad Cultural (the Cultural Society), which was led by newspaper publisher Luis G. Gasca, and Liga de Obreros y Campesinos (League of Workers and Peasants), a group consisting of 264 Mexicans and Mexican Americans, many of whom worked, or had worked, for Ford Motor Company. Rivera also used Gasca's newspaper, *La Prensa Libre,* to urge Mexicans and Mexican Americans to return to Mexico, and he mentored other Mexican and Mexican Americans in writing similar articles. For his part, Rivera often wrote that in a classless communist society people never went hungry and always had a place to call home.

Despite Rivera's efforts to convince the Mexican and Mexican American people of Detroit of the benefits of socialism and communism, a majority of them opted to leave Michigan not because they bought into Rivera's political beliefs but because Rivera promised them that the Mexican government would provide them with a plot of land,

Rivera and the Catholic Church

Taking note of Rivera's efforts was the Catholic Church of Detroit, which took offense at what he had to say. Catholic Church leaders accused him of using La Sociedad Cultural "to instill Soviet principles into 'Mexican souls,'" and La Prensa Libre as yet another means "to spread socialism among Mexicans."* Joining the Catholic Church in voicing their concerns with Rivera's methods and doctrine were a large majority of the Mexican and Mexican American population of Detroit, who wrote a letter to Catholic Bishop Gallagher admonishing Rivera for his beliefs and for having converted some of their neighbors to communism. Ardent Catholics found personal means by which they could counter what Rivera had to say. For example, Simón Muñoz founded the newspaper La Chispa, in which he denounced what Rivera was preaching.

*Dennis Nodín Valdés, *El Pueblo Mexicano en Detroit y Michigan* (Detroit: Wayne State University Press, 1982), 40; Skendzel, *Detroit's Pioneer Mexicans*, 10.

transportation into Mexico once they arrived at the Mexican border, and financial assistance until they could make it on their own.

Accepting their fate gracefully and with dignity were Mexicans like Ansel Moras, who during an interview at the Detroit Railroad Depot just prior to his departure stated, "The welfare was nice to us. They supported me and my wife and six children for over a year. But I did not want their charity, I wanted a job." Expressing similar sentiments were Miss Conception di Alday, who had "acquired a perfect knowledge of English," in hopes of securing a good position, and Fred Martino, a city worker who had been on government rolls for two years.[16]

Interestingly enough, aboard trains heading to Mexico were also women with names like Olidia Pintura, Alice Garcia, and Betty Mendess, Anglo-American women married to Mexican men, who, according to the *Detroit News*, "renounced their own country and left for Mexico, rather than desert their men."[17]

Also aboard these trains were Mexican women who had married Anglo-American men. However, in their case, their Anglo-American husbands were not allowed to accompany them back to Mexico on the same train. This meant that Anglo-American men married to Mexican women not only had to pay for their journey south, but in some cases were separated from their families. Such was the case with Leland Mallett, a Detroiter who met his wife while on business in San Luis Potosi. They married and moved to Detroit, where they started a family. Out of work, Mallett decided to take his family to Mexico, but he could not afford to pay his fare. He tried sneaking onto the train on which his family was riding. However, he was caught and kicked off, and as the train pulled away from the station, he waved goodbye to his family from the train platform.[18]

In describing the final departure of these people, *Detroit News* reporter S. L. A. Marshall wrote, "Michigan's separation from her Mexican colony is not a phase, but the closing of an epoch. There will be no such resurgence of the tide as occurred in 1922 and 1923, when better times brought thousands of laborers back to this country who had returned to Mexico during the slump of 1921."[19] When all was said and done an estimated 12,500 of the city's Mexicans returned to Mexico.

Only time could prove whether Marshall's prediction would hold true. However, for some of the Mexicans and Mexican Americans who voluntarily returned to Mexico, what awaited them was not the promised plot of land, transportation, and financial assistance, but hardship and despair. Most had to wait for a number of weeks before transportation was available to take them into Mexico, and they found that food was hard to come by. Once in Mexico, some received the plots of land promised them, while others were left to fend for themselves. Some remained in Mexico; however, most made a hasty retreat back into the United States.

The Mexicans and Mexican Americans who remained in Detroit during the Great Depression eked out a living the best they could. Men roamed the streets in search of scrap metal, or took work as laborers digging ditches, or paving roads, while women took part-time work as seamstresses and cleaning ladies. Some received government assistance, while others found work on projects undertaken as part of Roosevelt's New Deal. Even so, like many Detroiters around them, Mexicans and Mexican Americans lost their homes, automobiles, and furniture, anything of value that was purchased through installment

Migrant farm workers in Michigan load crated asparagus onto a truck. From here the produce will be transported to Midwestern markets. From their early arrival in Michigan until now, Mexican and Mexican-American migrant farm workers played a vital role in the success of Michigan's agricultural industry. Photograph by Refugio I. Rochín. Courtesy of Julian Samora Research Institute, Michigan State University.

plans, due to their inability to make payments. Some moved into cheaper housing, or in with relatives to ease the cost of living.

Overall, the Great Depression set back a Mexican and Mexican American community that had just been starting to come into its own. So devastating was the Great Depression on the Mexican and Mexican American population of Detroit that by 1936 the director of the U.S. Immigration Service estimated that there were only twelve hundred Mexicans living in Detroit.

Even so, the Mexicans and Mexican Americans who remained in Detroit managed to survive, and even made some progress during the 1930s. Attendance at Our Lady of Guadalupe Catholic Church remained steady, though its membership would continue to decline throughout the decade and the church would be closed in 1938. A Protestant church servicing Mexicans and Mexican Americans was founded in 1933. In that same year, the newspaper *El Atomo* (The Atom) made its debut. Published by Jose F. Alfaro, a one-time automotive plant worker, *El Atomo* remained in publication until 1935. It resurfaced in the fall of 1937, and this time lasted until the summer of 1938, when it was shut down for good. In 1936, the first Spanish-language radio program in the Detroit area was also founded by Alfaro. His radio program was broadcast on Saturday nights from 6:00 P.M. to 7:00 P.M. by the radio station WMBC. It consisted of live talent and music.

Despite these advances, the city of Detroit would not see an increase in its Mexican and Mexican American population until 1937, when the economic picture started to improve. By 1940 the number of Mexicans and Mexican Americans in Michigan rose to 3,694. This growth was spurred on by Michigan's growing position as the nation's leading producer of beans, pickles, fruits, and vegetables, and its more that 140,000 acres of sugar beets, requiring a workforce of over twenty thousand workers to care for them. This Mexican and Mexican American population was miniscule compared to that of 1930, yet it served to disprove those with dire predictions for the future of Mexicans in Detroit. Mexicans and Mexican Americans would return to the state, and with the start of World War II their numbers would grow to not only equal those of the past, but surpass them as well.

Resurgence of Michigan's Mexicans and Mexican Americans

With the resurgence and growth of Michigan's agricultural and industrial concerns in the late 1930s, Mexicans and Mexican Americans once again found their way to Michigan. Their arrival would mark the beginning of what would become the second great wave of Mexicans and Mexican Americans into Michigan. Across the Wolverine state the Mexican and Mexican American population began to grow. By 1940, the Mexican and Mexican American population of Saginaw stood at 455, that of Pontiac stood at 148, and that of Flint stood at 103. In the city of Detroit, the Mexican and Mexican American population rose to 1,565. Towns located near factories, such as Dearborn, Ecorse, Hamtramck, Highland Park, Lincoln Park, Wyandotte, and even an area in Detroit known as Delray, also saw a rise in the number of Mexicans and Mexican Americans living within their boundaries.

What distinguished the Mexicans and Mexican Americans who arrived in the state during the early 1940s from the first wave of early pioneers was that a majority of those entering the state at the start of the second wave traveled directly to the towns and cities of Michigan in order to secure a position in industry. The decision to do this was based not only on the fact that by now a number of Mexicans and Mexican

Americans were experienced in working in this sector, but also on the availability of jobs following the start of World War II.

The Mexicans and Mexican Americans who remained in Detroit during the Great Depression and the years that followed still lived in the vicinity of the Most Holy Trinity Church. A majority of the Mexicans and Mexican Americans returning to Detroit, and those coming to the city for the first time, also settled in that area.

With this boost to the city's Mexican and Mexican American population, the number of Mexican and Mexican American businesses increased, as did the number of mutual aid societies and cultural organizations, which became, and remain, a characteristic of the Mexican and Mexican American communities of Michigan. The Mexican and Mexican American businesses in the area included grocery stores, meat markets, drugstores, a doctor's office, and a lawyer's office. A 1940 flyer announcing the celebration of the Sixteenth of September listed a number of restaurants where celebrants could eat, including the Texas Restaurant, the Cervantes Café, El Rancho Grande, the Madrid Grill, the Mexico Restaurant, La Vencedora, El Chico, and the Monterrey Café. Bars and pool halls with names like, San Antonio, El Tenampa, Pardo's Bar, Lucky Clover Bar, and El Patio also grew in popularity.[20]

In 1940 Jose F. Alfaro founded a second Spanish-language radio program. Broadcasted on the radio station WJLB on Saturdays from noon to 1:00 P.M., the show lasted for two years. Cancellation of the show was not due to a lack of interest, but because after America's entrance into World War II the program could not be produced at a profit.

Adding to the number of Mexicans and Mexican Americans who came directly to the towns and cities of Michigan in the late 1930s, looking for work, as well as those who had remained in the state throughout the depression, were thousands of Mexicans and Mexican Americans who entered the state following America's entrance into World War II. A majority of these arrivals came to the state as part of the United States' Bracero program. Implemented in 1942, the Bracero program was seen as Mexico's part in aiding America's war effort.

Under the Bracero program, Mexicans were allowed to enter the United States in order to work the nation's farms and eventually its railroads. In the original agreement between the two countries, which took effect in July 1942, Mexicans were guaranteed wages at the going rate for at least 75 percent of a contract period, and the right to walk away from a contracted job, no questions asked. Standards were also set for the conditions under which Mexicans and Mexican Americans were to work. While these regulations looked good on paper, they were seldom implemented.

From 1942 to 1947 an estimated 200,000 Mexicans took advantage of this opportunity to come to the United States. The first year saw 4,000 men enter the country; this number grew to 52,000 the following year, and reached its peak in 1944, with 62,000 men crossing over. In the next three years this number would diminish to 30,000. As was the case during the first wave of Mexican and Mexican American immigration and migration to Michigan, some Mexicans and Mexican Americans left the fields in search of a better life in the towns and cities of Michigan. Mirroring a large number of the early Mexican and Mexican American pioneers of Michigan, most of those leaving the fields came to Detroit, where they settled in two primary areas. The first was the long-established area around Most Holy Trinity Church. The second was an area around Bagley Avenue, from Trumbull to West Grand Boulevard, which for the most part was served by St. Anne's Parish.

Encouraging the growth of these areas and the preservation of the culture and heritage of Mexico, as well as playing an important role in the religious lives of Mexicans and Mexican Americans were religious groups such as Los Caballeros de Cristo (Knights of Christ), Las Guadalupanas, Las Hijas de Mexico (The Daughters of Mexico), and Los Cusrillistas, a Christian movement organization. Supporting their efforts was Father Clement Kern, who was assigned to Most Holy Trinity Church in 1943. Father Kern was to endear himself to the Mexican and Mexican American people, eventually earning the nickname "El Padre Kern." Under his guidance, protests against the treatment of seasonal farm workers were undertaken, as was the creation of Casa Maria, a social agency that helped Mexican and Mexican American families adjust to life in Detroit.

In the years that followed, Padre Kern would also organize Corktown College, where students were taught how to speak and write

English, and given classes in citizenship. Classes in homemaking were also offered. In addition, a clinic was established within the school to assist those in need.[21] Taking note of the work of Padre Kern, the Detroit Board of Education set aside rooms in the Pitcher and Houghton Schools for the purpose of teaching English to Mexican and Mexican American children.

As the 1940s progressed, attendance at, and the overall Mexican and Mexican American population around, St. Anne's Catholic Church grew rapidly. The founder of Detroit, Antoine De La Mothe Cadillac, had established this church in 1701. Beginning in 1946, a Spanish Mass was celebrated in a side chapel for the older, non-English-speaking people of the community, while the younger, English-speaking Mexican and Mexican American parishioners were encouraged to attend the regular mass in the main church building. Three organizations were founded specifically to serve the needs of St. Anne's Catholic Church's Mexican and Mexican American members and the surrounding community: Los Caballeros Catolicos (Knights of Columbus), the Third Order of St. Francis, which was canonically erected in 1958, and Las Damas Católicas (the Catholic Ladies), a group that was first started in 1933 at Our Lady of Guadalupe Church. Interestingly enough, it was because of the pressure exerted on the pastor of St. Anne's by Los Caballeros Catolicos that a Spanish mass was offered at the church and a statue of the Mexican patron saint, La Virgen de Guadalupe, was allowed into the side chapel, where the Spanish-language mass was held.[22] Both of these concessions on the church's part went directly against the wishes of Cardinal Mooney, the archbishop of Detroit from 1937 to 1958, who had gone on public record as favoring no special treatment for the Mexican and Mexican American population of Michigan.

Perhaps the most significant of all Mexican and Mexican American groups established in Detroit during this time was the Mexican American Post #505 of the American Legion, which consisted of Mexican American veterans of World War II. Granted a charter by the American Legion, the chapter was organized in May 1946. The group, whose members were for the most part second-generation Mexicans, brought pride and a sense of belonging to the Mexican and Mexican American people of Detroit. After all, here was a group of men who had been among the more than 300,000 Mexican Americans from across the country who had fought and had been willing to lay down their lives to defend the American way.

Aside from the continuing tradition of forming mutual aid societies and cultural organizations for the betterment of the Mexican and Mexican American population of Detroit, Mexicans and Mexican Americans also kept alive the celebration of patriotic holidays. Helping to publicize the various cultural, patriotic, and religious events, as well as the news concerning the Mexicans and Mexican Americans of Detroit, was the Spanish radio program, Cantares de mi Pueblo (Songs of my town). Founded in 1948 by Roy Flores, the show was so popular that it remained on the air for over thirteen years, and eventually gained listeners throughout southeastern Michigan and Ohio.[23] The year 1948 also saw the rebirth of a newspaper serving the Mexican and Mexican American community, the first since 1933. The latest entry in the area of Mexican and Mexican American newspapers was called the *Union*. It was founded by members of El Comite Patriotico Mexicano, and it lasted two years.

By 1950, the Mexican and Mexican American population of Detroit stood at an estimated twenty-five thousand. Their numbers had also increased in Michigan towns such as Saginaw, Pontiac, and Flint, while the number of Mexicans and Mexican Americans living in rural communities had decreased. With this growth in the Mexican and Mexican American population in the towns and cities of Michigan, the continued presence of Mexicans and Mexican Americans in the Wolverine state was assured, and in the decades to come the Mexicans and Mexican Americans of Michigan would no longer be satisfied with simply maintaining a presence; they would become politically active in the hope of gaining a say in local, state, and national politics.

Stepping Out of the Shadows: El Movimiento

A s was the case from the onset of their arrival in Michigan, during the 1950s and 1960s, the Mexican and Mexican American people of Detroit maintained and gave birth to mutual aid societies and cultural groups concerned with aiding and enriching the lives of their people. Mexican and Mexican American businesses also continued to grow and prosper, as the Mexican and Mexican American population of Detroit grew from an estimated 25,000 in 1950 to over 32,000 by the end of the 1960s. Though this growth slowed somewhat during the era of McCarthyism in the 1950s, when Mexicans and Mexican Americans were deported not because of economic issues but rather because of issues of citizenship, with the immigration reforms of the 1960s the Mexican and Mexican American populations of Detroit and Michigan continued to increase. However, even with the deportations during the 1950s, by the start of the 1960s, Grand Traverse County had more migrant workers than did any other county in the country, and Michigan employed more migrant farm workers than any other state, excluding Texas. Predictably, a large number of these migrant farm workers left the fields as they became aware of the economic opportunities waiting for them in the towns and cities of Michigan. Many of them learned of these opportunities from family members with estab-   **39**

lished roots in Michigan. With the addition of these agricultural work-
ers to the relatively small population of Mexicans and Mexican
Americans already living in communities such as Adrian, Ecorse, Grand
Rapids, Lansing, Muskegon, Pontiac, Port Huron, and Wyandotte, the
Mexican and Mexican American communities in these towns began to
grow and take on a life of their own.

In Detroit, the Mexican and Mexican American population not
only maintained a presence in established neighborhoods but also
began to move from the original Michigan-Bagley areas to neighborhoods along Vernor Highway on the west side of Detroit. The major reason behind this shift in population just as the Mexicans and Mexican
Americans of Detroit were developing a sense of community lay in the
fact that the city of Detroit had initiated its Master Plan. For Mexicans
and Mexican Americans living west of Woodard Avenue, this meant that
their homes were razed to expand the central business district and to
add a freeway through the city. The demolition of homes in the area
greatly impacted the congregations of Ste. Anne and Most Holy Trinity.
In a book regarding the bicentennial anniversary of St. Anne's, the trau-
matizing event was described as follows: "The ball and chain swung
mercilessly and wiped out homes and families within three blocks of
the church. Many families were openly harassed to make way for trucks
while others were disheartened by the inevitability of so-called
progress. Freeways gouged deep into the life stream of the parish, forc-
ing unwilling families out."[24]

As early as 1955, the Mexican and Mexican American population
began to attend church services at a large Catholic Church named the
Holy Redeemer, which had been built in 1880 to serve the Irish and
German populations that had built up the southwest section of the city.

Holy Redeemer records indicate that by 1960 there were 200 chil-
dren of Mexican ancestry in the church's elementary school, of the 1,200
students. These records further indicate that by the following year, 500
of the church's members were of Mexican ancestry, and that a mass in
Spanish was instigated on their behalf. Attendance by Mexicans and
Mexican Americans also continued at St. Anne's and Most Holy Trinity.
Mexican and Mexican Americans could also be found at All Saints
Church on West Fort Street at Springwells Avenue and at the Holy Cross

Church, located in the Delray area. Still others attended St. Boniface, St. Vincent, St. Leo, and St. Anthony, all on Detroit's West Side.

Serving Protestant Mexicans and Mexican Americans was Primera Iglesia Bautista Mexicana (the First Baptist Mexican Church), which was founded in 1955. By 1960, the church's membership grew to include two hundred Mexican, Mexican American, and American families. Also in 1960 the congregation also started Primera Iglesia Bautista del Sur (First Baptist Church of the South), a mission of Lincoln Park Baptist Church.

Despite the addition of newcomers, the most striking feature of the Mexican and Mexican American population of Detroit at this time was the increased size of the second- and third-generation population, many of whom had been born in Michigan. Also unique to the time was the fact that a large percentage of these second- and third-generation Mexicans and Mexican Americans could be found working in the automotive plants of Ford Motor Company and Cadillac, or in steel factories and foundries, such as Kasel Steel, and not in the agricultural fields.

Keeping stride with the rise of Michigan's Mexican and Mexican American populations were newspapers such as *El Informador* (the Informer), which was founded in 1954 by Jose R. Flores and was published until 1956. Flores would follow this effort by buying *El Atomo* and changing its name to *Noticias* (News). The newspaper would stay in existence until 1958, when Professor Jose Elisandro, an educator from Monterrey, started *Ecos de Michigan* (Echoes from Michigan). This newspaper would stay in business for six months before being replaced by the weekly tabloid named *El Heraldo* (the Herald). *El Heraldo* would last until 1961, after which time Mexicans and Mexican Americans turned to out-of-state newspapers, such as *La Prensa, El Diario, El Norte, El Informador, La Opinion, Iniversal, Excelsior,* and *Novedades* for the news when a local provider was not in business.[25]

Leading the way in Spanish radio programming was Javier Cardenas, a Guadalajaran, who produced and directed a Spanish radio program on the radio station WPON in Pontiac, Michigan. Starting in October 1952, Cardenas's program aired for one hour on Saturdays and Sundays. The program would last until November 1954. In January of 1955, Cardenas moved the program to WPAG in Ann Arbor, where it aired until 1958. After this, it was picked up by WHRV in Ann Arbor, where it lasted until 1980. By this time the program played Monday through Friday, from 6:30 to 7:30 P.M., and on Saturdays from noon to 1:00 P.M. In 1961, Cardenas also produced and directed a program for WQTE of Monroe, Michigan. The program aired on Sundays from 10:00 to 11:30 A.M. From this location the program reached the Mexican and Mexican American populations of Detroit, Pontiac, Adrian, Toledo, and northwestern Ohio. At the heart of Cardenas's programming were stories designed to unite and inform the Mexican and Mexican American populations of Michigan and Ohio. Announcements were also made to inform them about upcoming patriotic and religious celebrations.[26]

Aside from expansion of Mexican and Mexican American radio programming, the year 1961 also brought the opening of the Alamo Theatre, a venue catering exclusively to the Spanish-speaking people of Detroit. The first such establishment in Detroit had been called the Aztec Theatre. It was located at Michigan Avenue and Brooklyn Streets. In the late 1950s, a second theatre had been established on Michigan Avenue and West Grand Boulevard. These theatres were part of a handful of entertainment venues reserved exclusively for the Spanish speaking population of Detroit, as well as for Spanish-speakers living in the surrounding area.

Mutual aid societies for the betterment of Mexicans and Mexican Americans also continued to emerge during this time. Such organizations included the youth group Club Camellia, which was founded in 1960, and the Comite de Festejos Guadalupanos (Committee of Guadalupe Parties), which was established in 1961. Some organizations, such as Los Caballeros Catolicos and the Mexican American Legion Post #505, solidified their place in the community at this time by acquiring their own buildings. Nothing, however, defined the history of the Mexican and Mexican American people of Detroit from the 1950s to the 1970s better than their involvement in politics, a development rooted in the union labor movement.

By the mid-1950s, a number of Mexicans and Mexican Americans working in factories throughout Michigan had joined fellow workers in forming labor unions. As union members, a segment of the Mexican and Mexican American workers received training in organizational skills. Before long, Mexican and Mexican American workers came to understand the power that came with organizing; so much so, in fact, that they organized fellow Mexican and Mexican American workers in an effort to get Mexican and Mexican American candidates elected into union offices. One of the early victories achieved by Mexican and Mexican American union leaders occurred at the Great Lakes Steel Corporation in Ecorse, where a bargaining block within the union assured the election of Mexicans and Mexican Americans as committeemen, grievance men, and shop stewards.[27]

Outside of the factories, Mexican and Mexican American union and community leaders founded an organization known as Latin Americans United for Political Action (LAUPA). The goal of this organization was to make politicians aware of the Mexican and Mexican American communities of Detroit, as well as to raise funds for local, state, and national Democratic candidates. Through the work of LAUPA members, candidates in mayoral and gubernatorial races, as well as for judgeships and in city council races, visited Mexican and Mexican American communities during parties or fiestas.

By the beginning of the 1960s, this early involvement in politics by the Mexican and Mexican American people of Detroit had given way to "patron politics," a form of politics in which a person becomes the self-appointed leader of a group of people. A majority of these leaders came from the ranks of men involved with labor unions. Sadly enough, a large number of these self-proclaimed leaders of the various neighborhoods did not consult with the people living in their neighborhoods when voicing their opinion on a particular issue; nor did they make any effort to organize their people into a voting block, or to educate them on issues involving their future. Even so, when asked for an opinion on any issue, the patron offered it up in the name of those living in his neighborhood. For politicians, a patron was a welcomed voice as long as he supported their stance on the issues; after all, in speeches or in interviews politicians with the backing of one or more patrons could claim to have the full support of the Mexican constituency of Detroit. Completely ineffective, this form of politics gained nothing but a few minor appointments for Mexicans and Mexican Americans, a situation that brought those individuals, and not the community, personal prestige.

Motivated in part by the political activism of men like Reis Tijerina and Corky Gonzales, as well as politically active groups such as the United Farmworkers, Movimiento Estudiantil Chicano de Aztlán (MEChA), La Raza Unida Party, the Young Lords, and the Brown Berets, and ultimately by the Detroit riots of 1967, the Mexicans and Mexican Americans of Detroit became personally involved in politics. Like the African Americans of Detroit, they took to the streets to protest neglect, mistreatment, and racism by the educational and public systems of the state.

To ease racial tensions and to begin the process of addressing the issues that led to the riots of 1967, city and industrial leaders formed New Detroit. This organization brought together Anglo-Americans and African Americans; no other ethnic group was represented. To counteract this lack of representation, Mexicans and Mexican Americans joined with citizens from other Latin American countries to form the Latino Caucus. This organization would provide a means by which the Latinos of Detroit could have a voice in politics, as well as in the formation of a number of agencies serving Latinos, such as the Chicano-Boricua Studies program at Wayne State University.

Permanent and migrant Mexican and Mexican American farmers also organized the "March for Migrants," which took place in March 1967. The March for Migrants was seventy miles long, starting in Saginaw and timed to end in Lansing on Easter Sunday. At least thirty statewide organizations supported their efforts, and the group received telegrams praising their efforts from César Estrada Chávez and the United Farm Workers Organizing Committee, as well as from United States Senators Phillip Hart and Robert Kennedy. In their petition of grievances, which was presented to Lieutenant Governor William Milliken, the group called for better wages, housing, and education, and for worker's compensation for migrant workers. Through these efforts attempts were made to correct discrepancies in each of these areas. Most importantly, the march served as a springboard for bringing both parties to the bargaining table, and for making the public aware of the treatment faced by the migrant workers of Michigan.

The following year saw the formation of the first Michigan chapter of La Raza Unida Party, a Mexican American political party whose goal was to unite Mexicans and Mexican Americans on a national level. In Michigan, organizers brought together groups such as the Circulo Mutualista, G.I. Forum, American Legion Post #505, Los Caballeros Catolicos, El Comite Patriotico, Las Cursillistas, and the Brown Berets. La Raza Unida Party met on the first Friday of the month in an effort to share concerns and to form strategies aimed to better the lives of Mexicans and Mexican Americans living in the state.

Also founded in 1968 was the Committee of Concerned Spanish-Speaking Americans (CCSSA), a grassroots group consisting of Mexican and Mexican American teachers, as well as local Mexican, Mexican American, Cuban, and Puerto Rican activists. The goal of the organization was to investigate educational problems and to make suggestions for correcting them. Through the efforts of this group the number of Latino teachers in Detroit grew, and money was allocated from the Detroit School Board to send a representative to the southwestern United States to recruit teachers. This concession, however, was short-lived when it did not prove beneficial to the Detroit school district. In 1971, CCSSA was also responsible for the introduction of a Spanish heritage class and a Latin American history class at a Detroit high school in which 17 percent of the students were of Latin American ancestry. The classes proved to be less than rewarding to students because unqualified personnel taught them. CCSSA's greatest contribution to the Spanish-speaking community of Detroit, however, was the sensitivity workshops the group initiated between Spanish-speaking mothers whose children attended Detroit schools and school administrators and teachers. In these workshops, Spanish-speaking mothers were able to voice their opinions on what and how things were being taught, and to provide input into course curriculums. It was largely because of the success of this program that Spanish-speaking mothers in Detroit became, and have remained, involved in their children's education.

In the public service arena, a milestone was reached by the Mexican and Mexican American people of Detroit with the formation of the group known as Latin Americans for Social and Economic Development (LA SED). The goal of the group was to form an institution that would deal with a variety of Chicano related issues. What made the formation of LA SED important was that it came about because a group of concerned Mexican and Mexican American Catholics came together to secure its funding from the Archdiocese of Detroit after the archdiocese announced in 1968 that it was allocating $1 million to programs aimed specifically at African Americans, and no other ethnic group. In reaction to the announcement, a core group of Mexican and Mexican American Catholics called a meeting attended by individuals representing twenty organizations. A steering committee was formed, and after a short time, a proposal to finance LA SED was drawn up and presented to the Archdiocese of Detroit. The proposal asked for $48,000, all of which was soon granted. LA SED became operational in April 1969 in a building located in downtown Detroit. The original staff consisted of a director, a full-time secretary, and two field representatives. Today, LA SED is still actively serving the Spanish-speaking community of Detroit, and its building is located in the heart of the Mexican barrio of Detroit.

Shortly after the launching of LA SED, a group of six people came together in an effort to establish an office within the Archdiocese of Detroit for the purpose of voicing and representing the needs of all Spanish-speaking people of Detroit. At the outset of their efforts, the group asked for a meeting with the bishop. Knowing of their cause, the bishop asked them to write a constitution for the office, a document citing the current needs of Spanish-speaking individuals, as well as a proposal for a Spanish-speaking office. With the assistance of the Human Relations Council for the Archdiocese, the requested information was prepared and submitted to the bishop. The proposal was rejected because there was simply not enough money to fund the office. Instead of giving up, however, the core group of activists brought together twenty Mexican and Mexican American individuals representing eight counties. They then asked again for a meeting with the bishop. In the meeting, these representatives presented their concerns and cited the number of Catholic Spanish-speaking people in the state. In June 1969, the Church approved what became known as the Latin American Secretariat. Officials staffing the office would be responsible to only the bishop. On 1 July 1969 the official Latin American Secretariat opened an office in downtown Detroit.

In the political sector, the growing influence of the Mexican and

Mexican American people of Detroit became apparent during the 1970 State Democratic Convention, which was held in Grand Rapids. At the convention, Mexican and Mexican American representatives ran a candidate for the board of governors at Wayne State University. The move caught everyone at the convention off guard; especially surprising was the unified front that the representatives exhibited. While the representatives knew that they did not have the votes needed to elect their candidate to the board outright, they certainly knew, as did everyone else in attendance, that they had the votes to affect the election.

In the end, the Mexican and Mexican American representatives to the convention threw their support behind two candidates willing to promote a proposal written by LA SED for a leadership- training program. In the long run, the strategy paid off when LA SED's proposal was funded by New Detroit, Inc., after it had received support from the Wayne State Board of Governors. With this funding in place, the leadership training program known as Latinos en Marcha (Latinos on the March) was implemented and placed under the leadership of a local Mexican American professor, who was teaching at Monteith College. Aside from leadership courses, as part of their training participants were required to take classes in Chicano history and culture, as well as social and political science, at Wayne State University. So successful was the program that after the first year students of Latinos en Marcha had established an educational information center at the LA SED building to assist any Latino who wanted to continue his or her education; established a scholarship fund; acquired radio air time at Wayne State University's WDET and had begun airing a weekly show entitled *El Grito De Mi Raza*. They also began planning for an in-depth written history of the barrio and its people. Finally, the group pushed through a Latino Studies Program at Monteith College, with permanent funding by Wayne State University, which admitted a minimum of thirty Latino students beginning in September 1973, and they pressured Wayne State University into hiring a Chicano recruiter.[28]

Most important, because of the combined efforts of the Mexican and Mexican American representatives at the 1970 state convention, LA SED, and the students of Latinos en Marcha, a Chicano studies program was eventually instigated at Wayne State University.

At Michigan universities such as Michigan State and the University of Michigan, Mexican and Mexican American students organized student groups with names like MEChA, Chispa, and United Mexican American Students. Mexican and Mexican American members of these groups spoke out in support of classes that focused on Chicanos, and they called for the recruitment of Spanish-speaking students and the hiring of Spanish-speaking teachers. While early efforts were successful, by the mid-1970s these groups had either died out or become complacent to the status quo.

As the 1960s came to a close, communities of Mexicans and Mexican Americans could be found throughout southwestern and southeastern Michigan. The radical decade of the 1960s had brought these groups a certain degree of political clout, and as the decade of the 1970s dawned, it seemed that the Mexicans and Mexican Americans of Michigan were poised to break into the political arena. The decade, however, would not see the emergence of a political machine. Instead, history shows that in the years that followed, the Mexicans and Mexican Americans of Michigan made tremendous strides in establishing themselves as a valuable piece of the rich fabric that made up the peoples of the Wolverine state.

The Coming of Age

By 1970, a large number of Mexicans and Mexican Americans lived in southwestern Wayne County, with settlements in the Tireman-Greenfield-Grand River section of Detroit as well as in the south-western part of the city. They also resided in Dearborn and the Downriver communities, as well as in Redford and Plymouth in Wayne County. There was an additional large concentration of Mexicans and Mexican Americans in Monroe County, with the highest density in the city of Monroe. Though sparse in number, Mexicans and Mexican Americans also resided in Ypsilanti, in Pontiac, and in the Armada-Capac area in both Macomb and St. Clair Counties. There was also a nucleus of Mexicans and Mexican Americans in the Hartland and Howell regions of Livingston County. In Detroit, the largest population of Mexicans and Mexican Americans lived between the Ambassador Bridge and Springwells, bounded on the north by Vernor Highway and on the south by the Detroit River.

State records indicate that by 1972, 27 percent of the Mexicans and Mexican Americans in Michigan had completed high school, and 3.6 percent had completed a four-year college education. The largest numbers of workers, 23.5 percent, were in the industrial trades, while 15.6 percent were craftsmen. A large number had moved into jobs in the clerical, sales, managerial, and professional categories. There was also a jump in the number of people coming into the state from South and Central America, which was a contributing factor to the formation of a Spanish-speaking middle class.

With the end of the radical 1960s, there emerged a pride in one's heritage and culture. This was true of people from a variety of backgrounds. This is not to say that pride in one's heritage and culture did not exist prior to the end of the 1960s, but that this pride was normally limited to private celebrations among people from the same ethnic background. However, the early 1970s saw an emergence of public celebrations that were accepted and welcomed by people from a variety of backgrounds and held at public venues, such as Patton, Riverside, and Clark Parks in Detroit. Participation in these celebrations now became multiethnic. For the Mexicans and Mexican-Americans of Michigan, public celebrations came to include El Día de los Muertos en Detroit (The Day of the Dead in Detroit), Fiestas Guadalupanas en Detroit (Lady of Guadalupe Celebration in Detroit), and Las Posadas en Detroit, which tells the story of Jesus' birth. Mexicans and Mexican-Americans also expressed themselves in barrio murals, in ballet *folklóricos,* in bilingual poetry, and in popular theatre based on the Teatro Campesino de Luis Valdez.

Entertainment venues serving the Spanish-speaking citizens of Detroit consisted of a number of night spots, including bars, lounges, and dance halls. The Stratford Theatre and Kramer Theatre featured "foreign language" films starring timeless Mexican film stars like Cantinflas, who was and is still best known to American audiences for his co-starring role in the film *Around the World in Eighty Days.*

Spanish radio shows now included a number of programs. For example, there was Una Serenata de Mi Barrio (A Serenade to My Neighborhood); Mananitas Mejicanos (Mexican Mornings); Los Latinos Americanos (The Latin Americans); Mejico Musical (Musical Mexico); La Hora de Olivia Galan (The Olivia Galan Hour); Musica, Alegria y Canciones (Music, Joy, and Songs); and the new college student-produced program called El Grito de Mi Raza (The Cry of My People). Radio stations catering to the Spanish-speaking people of Michigan included WAAM (16 FM), WIID (10.90 AM), WMZK (98 FM), and WQRS (105.1 FM).

In the area of commerce, a number of businesses belonging to the Spanish-speaking population of Detroit were found on Bagley, Vernor, Junction, Livernois, and Springwells. These businesses included specialty shops, restaurants, gift shops, and buildings housing the offices of community organizations. Mexican restaurants blossomed and prospered. Numbered among them were the Acapulco Restaurant, Armando's Taco House, El Sol Restaurant, the Hidalgo Restaurant, Las Palmas Restaurant, the Mexican Village, Rancho's Taco House, and the Xochimilco Restaurant. The names of many of these restaurants, as with early Mexican restaurants in Detroit, reflected the history of Mexico, as well as the region of Mexico from which the restaurant's fare originated.

The Spanish-speaking population of Detroit also established a number of markets catering to Spanish speakers. These included Alvarado's Super Market, La Esperanza, Super Mercado de María, and the Torres Market. Four factories producing Mexican food, including flour and corn tortillas, were also established.

Community organizations, some of which dated back decades, continued to offer assistance to the Spanish-speaking population of Detroit. Among these groups, which numbered about sixty-seven, were Los Caballeros Catolicos, Circulo Mutualista Mexicano, and El Club Artístico Femenino. Political, business, and social organizations also continued to organize the Spanish-speaking population of Detroit in an effort to form a united voice. Among these groups were La Raza Unida Detroit Chapter, Los Hispanos Unidos de Detroit, a G.I. Forum chapter, the Latin American Businessmen's Association, and LA SED.

By the mid-1970s, the Mexican and Mexican American citizens of the Wolverine state could no longer be ignored. During the presidential election of 1976, Jimmy Carter addressed a crowd of Mexicans and Mexican Americans at the El Union de Civica Mexicana in Saginaw as a part of their Diez y Seis de Septiembre celebration. He urged those present to vote for him and to get others registered to vote so they could vote for him as well. He predicted that with their support there was no way that native-son Gerald R. Ford would carry the state. It is interesting to note that while Carter was making this speech, Ford was delivering a speech at the same time to people gathered at the University of Michigan.

As the decade came to an end, the office of the United States Census announced that by 1980 the number of Spanish speakers in Michigan stood at 89,000. This rise in the number of Spanish speakers living in the state can be attributed to the fact that the census of 1980 grouped Mexicans and Mexican Americans with all individuals who chose to identify themselves as "Hispanics." Even so, it was estimated that 63 percent of those counted were Mexican, 12 percent were Puerto Rican, and 3 percent were Cuban. According to the census, Hispanics were concentrated in southeastern Michigan. Counties with the largest number included Wayne (46,301), Oakland (14,478), Genessee (7,469), Macomb (6,638), Ingham (10,523), and Kent (8,742). Other counties having Hispanic residents included Saginaw, Oceana, and Lenawee, where they made up more than 5 percent of the county's total population.

In Detroit, most Mexicans and Mexican Americans remained concentrated in the southwest part of the city, beginning in the Hubbard-Richard neighborhood near the Ambassador Bridge and continuing to the Rouge River. However, time did see some expansion of African Americans and Anglo-Americans into neighborhoods in the Vernor-Junction area, so that several neighborhoods had significant numbers of Anglo-Americans, African Americans, and Hispanics living together.

While the Mexicans and Mexican Americans of Michigan continued to be involved in the state's agricultural and manufacturing industries, by 1980 more and more Mexicans and Mexican Americans were moving into managerial, professional, and technical positions. State educational records indicate that at this time 27 percent of Michigan's Hispanics had no high school diploma, while 28 percent had completed a high school education; 21 percent had some college education; 6 percent had an Associate's degree; 10 percent had a Bachelor's degree, and 8 percent had a graduate degree.

In the area of commerce, the number of Hispanic-owned firms rose from 1,616 in 1982 to 2,654 by 1987. Of this number, Mexicans and Mexican Americans owned 1,704. Half of these businesses were in the service industries, 17.37 percent were involved in the retail trade, and 10.98 percent were involved in construction. The rest owned businesses dealing with transportation, finance, insurance, real estate, agriculture, manufacturing, and industry.

Hispanic Income in Michigan, 1990

$0 to $9,999	19%
$10,000 and $19,999	14%
$20,000 to $29,999	14%
$30,000 to $39,999	11%
$40,000 to $49,999	12%
$50,000 to 59,999	9%
$60,000 to $74,999	10%
$75,000 to $99,999	6%
$100,000 or more	5%

Aside from the strides made in the area of education, income, and commerce, the Mexican and Mexican American population of Detroit also continued to showcase its culture and heritage. The year 1985 saw the first parade in southwest Detroit celebrating Mexico's independence. Two years later, Aquinas College of Grand Rapids and Dos Manos (Two Hands) in Royal Oak presented the first public exhibit focusing on a Mexican celebration. In this instance it centered around El Día de los Muertos (The Day of the Dead), a Mexican ritual honoring the dead that takes place on the second of November. Others dealing with the same topic followed this breakthrough exhibit. In 1989 La Casa de la Unidad de las Artes Culturales and Media Center hosted an exhibit on the Day of the Dead. Similar exhibits were then hosted by the DePree Art Center at Hope College in Holland and at the Pontiac Creative Arts Center. The pinnacle was reached in 1991, when the Detroit Institute of the Arts hosted an exhibit on the Day of the Dead that was created by the Mexican and Mexican American population of Michigan.

As 1987 came to an end, the Hispanic population in the United States stood at 18.8 million. This meant that 4.3 million more Hispanics resided in America now than had only seven years prior. In Michigan. it also became evident that the majority of the state's Hispanics were relatively young. The U.S. Census of 1990 reported that 0.9 percent of the state's Hispanics were age sixty-five and over; 0.8 percent were over

eighty-five, and 95 percent were under sixty-five. By 1996, it was estimated that Hispanics and Asians were the fastest growing minority
groups in Michigan. As reported in the 19 December 1997 issue of the
Detroit Free Press, Asians and Hispanics were "lured to Detroit by the
promise of jobs and affordable housing." Oakland County became
home to 35,597 Asians, a quarter of the state's Asian population, while
Wayne County added 55,885 Hispanics to its existing population. A
large number of these people were drawn to the state from Mexico,
Central America, California, and Texas. Most of these newcomers settled in southwest Detroit, where a network of stores, churches with
bilingual Masses, and support services were found.

In the area of commerce, the 1990s witnessed the emergence of a
number of Hispanic-owned businesses, such as Uni Boring Company,
Inc., Gonzales Design Group, and Ideal Steel and Builders' Supplies. In
1996, these three companies came together to open the Hispanic
Manufacturing Center in the City of Detroit's Empowerment Zone.
Located in the former General Motors Cadillac Plant in downtown
Detroit, the companies use the plant for production of their products.
Most importantly, the facility provides work for people living in south-
west Detroit. These companies also became invaluable to the Detroit
community by sponsoring and supporting a number of social pro-
grams, such as "Youth at Risk" and "GRACE," which stands for Gang
Retirement and Continuing Education, a program that aids ex-gang
members in securing jobs at the Hispanic Manufacturing Center.
During the 1990s, a number of mainstream businesses were established
in southwest Detroit, including Murrays' Auto Parts, Hollywood Video,
McDonald's, Burger King, Rite Aid Pharmacy, and CVS Pharmacy.

Sadly enough, 1994 saw the passing of Hank Aguirre, the founder of
Mexican Industries, a company that produced automotive parts. A former major league baseball player and Tiger pitcher, Aguirre started the
company in southwest Detroit in 1979 with eight employees and a ware-
house located on Eighth and Bagley. At the time of his death the company had 1,200 employees and sales of more than $120 million a year.
Upon his death, the company was passed on to his four children and
was led by one of his daughters, Pamela, until the business closed in
2001 due to a number of circumstances.

As part of its celebration of El Día De Los Muertos, the Chicano/Latino Studies Program Speaker Series at Michigan State University honors Michigan's Chicano workers from a multitude of areas. The altar above was exhibited during the 1998 celebration. Dr. Javier Pescador prepared it in honor of betabeleros (beet workers). Photograph courtesy of Julian Samora Research Institute, Michigan State University.

The 1990s witnessed significant growth in the areas of entertainment and news, and Mexicans and Mexican Americans operated radio stations over customary airwaves and on the Internet. In Detroit, *El Central*, a bilingual newspaper founded in the late 1980s and operated by Dolores Sanchez, served the Mexican and Mexican American community, and there were a number of other bilingual newspapers founded throughout the state. However, *El Central* is now the only bilingual newspaper in the state published on a weekly basis. Ms. Sanchez also publishes the Michigan Hispanic Directory, a listing of Mexican, Mexican American, Latino, and Hispanic businesses, mutual aid societies, and organizations, as well as businesses that offer products produced by Mexicans, Mexican Americans, Latinos, and Hispanics.

On Michigan's college campuses, programs focusing on Mexicans, Mexican Americans, Latinos, Hispanics, and Chicanos have been implemented, and celebrations surrounding the culture and history of Mexicans, Mexican Americans, Latinos, and Hispanics have become expected yearly events. On some college campuses, such as Eastern Michigan University, monuments have even been erected to honor Mexican Americans, Latinos, and Hispanics who have contributed in a significant way to the history of the United States. For example, in Eastern Michigan University's case, a water fountain honors César Estrada Chávez, the founder of the National Farm Workers Association.

Continuing to shine as the Midwest's premiere Hispanic research center, undertaking research on issues of relevance to the social, economic, and community development of Hispanics, is the Julian Samora Research Institute (JSRI). Established in 1989 at Michigan State University and named for Dr. Julian Samora, a pioneer in Mexican American studies as well as a professor of sociology at Michigan State University and then at Notre Dame, JSRI is the only Latino research center at a major university in the Midwest. Some of the institute's primary interests include the areas of labor, income, poverty, immigration, migration, and transnational connections, as well as family, elderly, youth, and gender issues.[29]

In the political arena, in 1998 the first Spanish-surnamed individuals were elected to represent districts in Lansing. These two people were Representative Belda Garza, a Democrat representing the Detroit/River Rouge area, and Valde Garcia, a Republican from St. Johns, who was later elected state senator in a runoff to fill the position after Mike Rogers was elected to the United States Congress in March 2001. In cities such as Detroit, Pontiac, and Lansing, a few Mexican Americans, Latinos, and Hispanics were also elected to public office, and a few garnered political appointments. Governor John Engler even appointed Mexican Americans, Latinos, and Hispanics to a variety of positions, such as the state Tax Tribunal, and Isidore Torres was appointed to the Wayne County Circuit Court. When the governor was criticized for not doing enough to appoint Mexican American, Latino, and Hispanic judges, Engler's spokesman, John Truscott, responded that the governor's office challenged critics "to provide us with good quality names that make it past the bar qualifications. We have to have names. We just can't create people."[30] True to this philosophy, when qualified individuals were presented to the governor's office, the governor made every effort to have them appointed to the Michigan court system. For example, at present two additional Latinos serve in the Michigan court system, including Judge Maria Luisa Oxholm, the first Latina to serve as a judge in the Thirty-Sixth District.

While these political gains are significant, as a whole political analysts maintain that the Mexican Americans, Latinos, and Hispanics of Michigan are too spread out to form voting blocks capable of electing a large number of Mexican Americans, Latinos, and Hispanics to public office. It is the belief of these political analysts and selected Mexican, Mexican American, Latino, and Hispanic leaders in Michigan that the only way for Mexican Americans, Latinos, and Hispanics to make significant political gains is to form alliances with Anglo-American and African American people. This must be a grassroots effort, where the individual Mexican American, Latino, or Hispanic has earned the trust and the respect of his or her neighbors first; then the community at large will follow from this epicenter of support. Aside from geographical barriers, political analysts also believe that Mexican Americans, Latinos, and Hispanics are kept from becoming politically active because of issues such as "poverty, language barriers, and the challenges of fitting into the mainstream."[31] This assessment holds especially true for newly arrived immigrants, who in many ways find themselves in the same circumstances faced by the early Mexican and Mexican American pioneers in Michigan.

The Mexican and Mexican American population of Michigan has stepped to the forefront in grassroots efforts to address educational issues concerning their children. For example, in July 1999, the Mexican, Mexican American, Latino, and Hispanic community of Lansing organized a march to bring about an awareness of the poor performance of Mexican American, Latino, and Hispanic children on the Michigan Educational Assessment Program examination, as well as the language barriers and high dropout and truancy rates in the Lansing School District. On Michigan's college campuses, Spanish-speaking student groups have stepped to the forefront in support of affirmative action and of the right of student groups to have access to university or college buildings that were in the past reserved for an elite few.

Thanks to their diligent work ethic throughout the 1970s, 1980s, and 1990s, the Mexicans and Mexican Americans of Michigan managed to move into jobs outside of the fields and factories. The number of those receiving high school diplomas and college degrees soared, as did the number of those establishing their own businesses. After the census of 1990 showed that most of Michigan's Hispanic population was under sixty-five years of age, the future seemed encouraging for Michigan's Mexicans and Mexican Americans in a number of areas, including politics, business, and education. Yet, while some advancements have been made in these areas, they are limited to a select few who have the contacts and the financial means by which to move ahead. Exactly what impact the advancements made by Spanish-speaking politicians, business owners, and educators will have on the Mexican and Mexican American population of the Wolverine state, it is too early to tell. However, as has always been the case with the Mexican and Mexican American population of Michigan, those that have will never forget those that do not. This is to say that when a need or a challenge facing the Mexican and Mexican American population of Michigan has been identified, Michigan's Mexican and Mexican American citizens have pulled together to address and solve the problem.

The New Millennium: The Promise of Tomorrow

The U.S. Census of 2000 showed that for the first time in the history of the United States, Hispanics were the largest minority group.[32] In the Michigan counties of Washtenaw, Livingston, Oakland, Macomb, and Wayne the number of Hispanics grew from 38,415 in 1980 to 107,467 by the year 2000. In Detroit, the 2000 census showed that 47,165 Hispanics resided in the city, which meant that they made up 5 percent of the city's population. In Grand Rapids, the Hispanic population rose from 9,394 in 1990 to 25,818 in 2000. Statewide there was a 61 percent increase in the Hispanic population, most of which was attributed to the large number of legal Mexican immigrants coming into the state, primarily from the Mexican cities of San Ignacio, Jesus Maria, and Arandas. This statistic points to the fact that Michigan is today undergoing its third great wave of Mexican immigration into the state. This means that these people are the first in a new generation of Mexicans in Michigan, the effect of which will not be known for a few years.

Overall, Michigan has more Hispanics than most other states, ranking fifteenth among the fifty states. Demographers have attributed the reasons for the arrival of these immigrants to better wages and schools, a chance to gain a college education for their children, or a chance to start a small business. Others came to join family members already established in the state in what is commonly referred to as chain migration. Today, there are so many Spanish-speaking people in northern Macomb and central Oakland counties that Spanish-speaking Masses at the Catholic churches are commonplace. Few of these newcomers are migrant workers, according to demographers. Instead, they are people who want to establish permanent roots, people who want to find work in manufacturing, in industry, or with residential or commercial construction companies. Of course, there are cases of illegal immigrants who struggle to make ends meet, and who are taken advantage of by their employers. Some leave, vowing never to return. Even so, there is an old saying among the Latinos of Detroit: "*Ya que preba la agua de Detroit, regresa uno*" (Once you taste the water of Detroit, you always come back.)."[33]

The future of Mexicans and Mexican Americans in Michigan looks promising as a new century dawns. Aside from those gains already mentioned, at the 2000 Democratic Convention in Los Angeles, the Michigan contingent included four Hispanic delegates and one Hispanic committee member. Since the turn of the millennium, political leaders and community activists have lobbied for affordable housing and more bilingual police, as well as more say in state politics and civil rights. They have pulled together with the goal of placing a Latino on the board of Detroit's branch of the National Association for the Advancement of Colored People. There has also been an effort to encourage patronage of Latino-owned businesses by the Detroit branch's Buy in Detroit program. Michigan's universities continue to embrace and cosponsor events celebrating the culture and heritage of their Mexican and Mexican American students. For example, in May 2000, Michigan Technological University, which is located in the Upper Peninsula, joined forces with the Hispanic student organization Nosotros (Us) and Michigan Tech's Educational Opportunity Outreach and Multiethnic Programs Division to sponsor the first ever Cinco de Mayo celebration held at the campus. The event featured guest speakers, tours, a piñata-making demonstration, and a folk fiesta with the Mariachi Cora musicians. One of the guest speakers was William Cruz of Lucent Technologies, who delivered a presentation entitled "Differences in Communication Styles between Latinos and Anglos." The

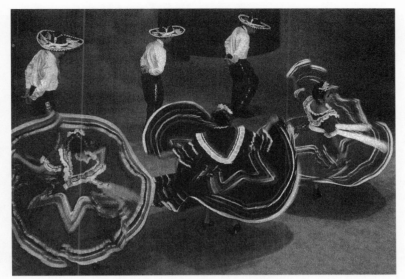

*Folklorico dancers add to the festivities commemorating Cinco de Mayo at
Michigan State University. Events similar to this have been a part of the cultural
life of Michigan's Mexicans and Mexican Americans since their early arrival in the
Wolverine state. Photograph courtesy of Julian Samora Research Institute,
Michigan State University.*

talk centered on the verbal and nonverbal communication styles of the
two groups, and how these styles can cause misperceptions and misin-
terpretations, which in turn can result in misunderstanding.

On the cultural front, an annual Hispanic Celebration at the State
Capitol began in 1999. The main organizers for the 2001 event were state
senator Valde Garcia and state representative Belda Garza. The event is
held on the lawn of the State Capitol. In 2001, an education summit on
ways to curb the dropout rate among Hispanic high school students
initiated the celebration. Later in the day, food venders provided lunch
while attendees enjoyed the salsa beat of Ozzie Rivera's band, a group
from southwest Detroit. State government leaders also issued procla-
mations in support of Michigan's Hispanic community, and special
honors went to Saginaw police officers Cari and Joaquin Guerrero and
their police dogs, Rookie and Felony, for their heroic rescue efforts at
the World Trade Center following the tragedy of September 11. The cel-

ebration ended with an awards presentation inside the Capitol Rotunda. Awards were presented in categories that included Outstanding Hispanic Education Award, Outstanding Hispanic Business/ Economic Development Award, Outstanding Hispanic Arts Award, Outstanding Hispanic Advocate/Civic Duty Award, Outstanding Youth Leadership Award, and Outstanding Hispanic Lifetime Achievement Award. As to the role the celebration plays in the life of Hispanics, state representative Belda Garza stated, "It is important that Hispanic people gather at the State Capital, not only to celebrate our culture and our achievements, but also to remind state government leaders that Hispanics have growing political clout. The Hispanic Heritage event grows every year, and serves as a reminder that our issues matter and deserve the attention of the Governor and the Legislature."[34]

Hispanics of Detroit hold a month-long celebration, starting on 15 September and ending on 15 October in honor of six Central American countries that received their independence from Spain. On 15 September, Independence Day is celebrated for Costa Rica, El Salvador, Guatemala, Honduras, and Nicaragua, and on 16 September it is celebrated for Mexico. El Día de la Raza (The Day of the People), a celebration of the heritage of Indian indigenous peoples in Latin America, rounds out the celebrations on 12 October. Likewise, El Día de los Muertos (The Day of the Dead) is also observed, and during the summer the Mexicans and Mexican Americans of Detroit celebrate their heritage as a part of Detroit's Ethnic Festival, an event that showcases the various ethnic groups residing in the city.

Leading the way in organizing annual cultural events, as well as fostering the continued economic development and growth of the Hispanic community of southwest Detroit, is the Mexicantown Community Development Corporation (Mexicantown CDC). Mexicantown CDC is led by Maria Elena Rodriguez. The organization is a not-for-profit, Michigan, 501(c)(3) corporation formed in 1989. Its mission includes the promotion of the Mexicantown restaurant, shopping, and cultural district across southeastern Michigan, supporting cultural programs and activities that educate and enrich the lives of residents of the neighborhood and the southeast Michigan region, as well as making physical improvements and performing maintenance in the Mexicantown

At a cost of $12.5 million, Mexicantown Community Development Corporation's International Welcome Center and Mercado provides a permanent venue for economic and cultural development in the heart of Detroit's Spanish-speaking population. Image courtesy of Mexicantown Community Development Corporation.

district, including parks and streetscapes. The organization's mission also includes entrepreneurial training and incubation to increase the economic self-sufficiency of neighborhood residents, and the reuse of vacant land and development of the Mexicantown International Welcome Center and Mercado.

In the area of cultural programs and activities, in 2002 Mexicantown CDC sponsored four events. These included a Cinco de Mayo Fiesta, an Irish-Mexican Fiesta, a Summer Mercado, and the eighth annual Día de los Muertos. Aside from these efforts, the organization is pushing ahead to make the Mexicantown International Welcome Center and Mercado a reality. The $12.5-million structure is located at Bagley Avenue and Twenty-first Street; a site in the heart of Mexicantown and at the base of the Ambassador Bridge to Windsor, Canada. When completed, the center will provide Mexicantown CDC with the opportunity to greet international visitors as they enter the city, state, and nation, and will optimize Mexicantown's identity as a tourist and entertainment destination within the city of Detroit. The project's four major components will include a State of Michigan Welcome Center, a Mexicantown Mercado, a retail and office building, and a public plaza. It will bring eighty-four new businesses and 190 new jobs to Mexicantown. The center will also offer cultural and arts programming within the Mexicantown Mercado and in the public plaza. Most important, the Mexicantown International Welcome Center and Mercado will honor the rich history of Latinos in the city and state while creating a more prosperous future for its vibrant, diverse, and historical neighborhood.

Aside from the work being done at Mexicantown CDC, the Spanish-speaking residences of southwest Detroit are served by La Casa de la Unidad de las Artes Culturales and Media Center (La Casa de la Unidad). Established in 1981, the nonprofit organization's mission is to provide southwest Detroit and other communities with the best available resources and programs which discover, develop, celebrate, and advance the Hispanic/Latino arts, its humanistic and spiritual values and its traditions, with respect for all. Programs and activities sponsored by La Casa de la Unidad include art exhibits featuring various artists throughout the year, poetry readings, workshops in photography, writing, art, graphics, printing, and publishing services, as well as a number of youth art programs. La Casa de la Unidad also works closely with Michigan State University Museum and the Michigan Humanities Council in producing documentaries regarding Michigan's Spanish-speaking residents. Humanities projects are also developed and produced in collaboration with the Walter Reuther Library and Wayne State University.

Representative of the cultural events produced by La Casa de la Unidad is the Unity in the Community Festival, an annual event that dates back to 1979. Drawing an average of eighteen thousand participants a year, the festival brings together people of all ages and from all sectors of the community for two days in September in order to celebrate two historical days, the Mexican Independence Day and the "Grito de Lares," an important date in the struggle for Puerto Rico's independence. Celebrated in historic Clark Park in southwest Detroit, the event is supported by over ten corporate sponsors, and over sixty businesses and agencies directly participate in the festival annually. Retail and marketing opportunities for businesses are also available.

The annual "Unity in the Community Festival" is produced by La Casa de la Unidad de las Artes Culturales and Media Center in Detroit, Michigan. The festival celebrates Mexico's independence, and the "Grito de Lares," an important event in the struggle for Puerto Rico's independence. Photograph by Bob McKeown and courtesy of Casa de Unidad Cultural Arts and Media Center.

Assisted by an estimated one hundred and fifty volunteers from the community, the festival features traditional and contemporary entertainment, employs over one hundred artists, conducts educational workshops in musical arts and dance, and serves as a showcase for local performing artists by widening their exposure.

Aside from the Unity in the Community Festival, La Casa de la Unidad also produces a Día de los Muertos observance in the month of November. The organization has also published a number of books by and about the Spanish-speaking residents of southwest Detroit. For example, the organization's book, *Fiesta, Fe, y Cultura*, which was copublished by the Michigan State University Museum and written by Laurie Sommers, is a well-crafted book that examines the celebration of El Día de los Muertos, Las Fiestas Guadalupanas, and Las Posadas in southwest Detroit.

The Mexican and Mexican American citizens of Michigan vary in lifestyle and economic circumstances, from migrant workers to upper-class professionals. Many Mexicans and Mexican Americans have put their children through college, own businesses, and contribute actively to the communities where they live. Yet, there are still many Mexicans and Mexican Americans struggling in the fields of Michigan, toiling hard in our rich soil to create a better life for themselves and their children. Regardless of their position in life, the Mexicans and Mexican Americans of Michigan are an important and growing population of the state.

The U.S. Census of 2000 revealed that the growth of Michigan's non-white and Hispanic population grew from 17.7 percent of the state's population in 1990 to 21.4 percent in 2000. Of minority groups, Hispanics accounted for the largest gain, growing from 201,397 in 1990 to 323,877 in 2000, an increase of a staggering 61 percent. If current trends continue, the number of Hispanics calling Michigan home will continue to skyrocket. Exactly how many of these people will be born in the state and how many will migrate or immigrate, cannot be anticipated. However, regardless of how or why they come to Michigan, once here, they will take their place among a group of Mexican and Mexican American people who have helped to shape as well as add to the ever-changing fabric that makes up the Wolverine state.

Early Mexican and Mexican American Organizations

Anahuac: Founded in 1926 by dissenting members of the Circulo Mutualista, the group sponsored social functions such as dances and dinners. Members aided Comite Patriotico in staging Fiestas Patrias. The group disbanded in the 1930s.

Archicofradía Guadalupana: This organization originated at the Most Holy Trinity Church in the Archdiocese of Detroit. It was dedicated to La Virgen de Guadalupe.

Chapultepec: Woman's club of unmarried girls. The organization sponsored social activities and dances. Especially active in 1930s, members helped during the Fiestas Patrias. The group disbanded in 1935.

Chihuahuenses Unidos: Membership of this group consisted of immigrants from the state of Chihuahua, Mexico. Formed in 1930, the group was extremely active during the 1940s. It was a social club that occasionally held dances.

Círculo Mutualista Mexicano: The leading Mexican society in Detroit. It was established in 1922, and served as a social, cultural, and self-help relief organization. Membership consisted of the elite of the colony that held white-collar and professional jobs.

Club Artístico Femenino: Founded to perform folkloric dances. This group was led by María Hernández Alcalá, and was most active during the 1940s.

Comisión de Festejos Guadalupanos: A committee made up of Guadalupanians representing a variety of churches. It raised funds for the Fiestas Guadalupanas held yearly in Detroit. The group's name was later changed to the Comité de Festejos.

Comité Círico y Patriótico Mexicano: One of several civic and patriotic groups that took on the organization of the Fiestas Patrias in Detroit. It was founded in the 1930s.

Cruz Azul: Achieved greatest time of activity during the 1920s. It was the ladies' auxiliary to the Círculo Mutualista.

Damas Católicas: Established within Our Lady of Guadalupe Church in 1933 by Father Luis Castillo with the purpose of doing charitable work and caring for the sick. It succeeded the Cruz Azul.

Hacheros del Mundo: Founded by G. C. López in 1939, this was an insurance society with a Spanish-speaking chapter in Detroit. One of its activities was sponsoring dances and other social functions for its members.

Latin American Club: Club formed in 1920 to provide cultural and social activities for the 168 students from Latin America that Ford Motor Company brought here to learn business. It ceased to exist in 1923. A club called Centro Español sprung off from this organization, and was open to all the Spanish-speaking people in Detroit.

Liga de Obreros y Campesinos: Founded in part by Diego Rivera in Detroit in 1932 to assist Mexicans with the repatriation program. The group disbanded in 1933, after Rivera left Detroit. A large percentage of the people this group assisted were left stranded in Laredo, Texas. The money supposedly given to officials there to assist returning Mexicans was apparently misappropriated.

Liga Filarmónica Mexicana: Promoted Mexican music in Detroit. It was founded in 1932.

Mexican American Post #505 of the American Legion: A veterans group composed of World War II soldiers. The group organized in May 1946, and at one point held meetings at the Neighborhood House on Porter and 4th Street. The organization sponsored social activities that took place in rented halls. In 1958, the group purchased a building at Cicotte and Denis Streets. It was the first Mexican American organization to own its own hall. In 1961 there were still seventy-five active members doing charitable work among the Spanish-speaking people of Detroit.

Northside Athletic Recreation Club: Founded in Lansing, Michigan, in 1970 for young Mexicans and Mexican Americans interested in practicing and participating in sports.

Obreros Unidos Mexicanos: Founded in 1926. Among its activities, the group assisted in the Fiestas Patrias. The organization was said to have received financial support from Diego Rivera. After encountering internal difficulties, a splinter group broke away to form the American Aztec Club.

Padres de Familias: Different from the group in Dearborn, this society was founded in Detroit as a part of Our Lady of Guadalupe Church. The organization was a member of El Comite Patriotico Mexicano. Father Luis Castillo founded the group in 1926. The chief aim of the organization was to secure a Catholic education for parents wishing this for their children. The group eventually became inactive as attendance at the church fell.

Sociedad Católica de San José: Founded by Simon Muñoz, this group was active from 1929 through the 1930s. The organization's main objective was providing religious instruction to Mexican children in public schools. The organization also held social functions for members. Originally, the group was associated with the Catholic Church.

Sociedad Católica Mexicana: Detroit's first Mexican society. Father Juan Pablo Alanís founded the organization in 1920 with the purpose of raising funds for a new church building, as well as the development of the cultural life of Detroit's Mexicans and Mexican Americans. The group succeeded in its fund-raising efforts, which led to the construction of Our Lady of Guadalupe Church. The group was disbanded after the church was completed.

Sociedad de Emilio Carranza: Consisted of people living in the southern part of Dearborn. Most of the group's members worked for Ford Motor Company. The organization was named after a young aviator killed in 1928. Most members hailed from the State of Coahuila, the birthplace of the aviation hero. The group died out in 1930, and was supplanted by Padres de Familias. The organization rented a room in the Salina School in Dearborn to teach Spanish to both adults and children.

Sociedad Guadalupana: The name used by a variety of organizations founded in each of the Catholic Churches serving Mexicans and Mexican Americans. Originally, these groups consisted mostly of the older Mexicans and Mexican Americans living in southwest Detroit. Meeting on a monthly basis, one of the goals of these groups was the organization of the Mexicans and the Mexican Americans attending a given parish, as well as the implementation of a mass in Spanish if the church did not already offer such an option.

Sociedad Mutualista de Ignacio Zaragosa: The first social and civic group founded in Lansing, Michigan. The organization honored Ignacio Zaragosa, the Mexican hero who with his troops defeated French invaders on 5 May 1867. Active in the 1940s, the group organized the celebration of El Diez y Seis de Septiembre. When the group took charge of celebrating all of Mexico's patriotic holidays, it changed its name to El Comite Patriotico Mexicano.

Mexican and Mexican American Pioneers

Alanis, Father Juan Pablo: The first priest to serve the members of Our Lady of Guadalupe Church. He established Sociedad Católica Mexicana, Detroit's first Mexican society, in 1920, for the purpose of raising funds for a new church building, as well as the development of the cultural life of Detroit's Mexicans and Mexican Americans. The group succeeded in its fund-raising efforts, which led to the construction of Our Lady of Guadalupe Church. The group was disbanded after the church was completed. Father Alanis left Detroit in 1927 and went to Rome.

Alfaro, Jose F.: A printer. Published *El Atomo*. He changed the name of the newspaper to *Noticias* in 1956. The newspaper remained in existence for three years. He also printed most of the early Mexican and Mexican American newspapers of Detroit. In 1936 he founded the first Spanish-language radio program in the Detroit area. It was carried by WMBC. It consisted of live talent and music. He was a self-educated man, who worked as an autoworker in Detroit. He sponsored dances and created Christmas cards that were extremely popular.

Benjamin, Charles C.: A Panamanian, he served in Detroit as the consulate for the Republic of Honduras. He was active in the welfare of

Detroit's Mexican colony, and served as an attorney for the Mexican Consulate of Detroit. He often defended the Spanish-speaking population of Detroit in court, and assisted Rivera in organizing a volunteer service for repatriation. He was to write a small volume in Spanish explaining the major legal rights and laws in the United States of America.

Cardenas, Javier: A native of Guadalajara, Cardenas produced and directed a number of Spanish radio programs. His first program premiered on the radio station WPON in Pontiac, Michigan, in 1952, and lasted until 1954. In the years to come, Spanish radio programs produced and directed by Cardenas aired on radio stations servicing Ann Arbor, Detroit, Adrian, Toledo, and northwestern Ohio. At the heart of Cardenas's programming were stories designed to unite and inform the Mexican and Mexican American populations of Michigan and Ohio. Announcements were also included to inform them about upcoming patriotic and religious celebrations.

Castillo, Father Luis: The second priest to serve the members of Our Lady of Guadalupe Church. He came to Detroit in December 1926 and remained until 1938. He was a native of Venezuela and was in his late twenties when he arrived in Detroit. He founded the organization Padres de Familias (Fathers of Families) at Our Lady of Guadalupe Church. The group's chief aim was securing a Catholic education for children whose parents wished them to have one.

Flores, Roy: Producer and founder of the Spanish radio program *Cantares de mi Pueblo* (Songs of my town). Established in 1948, the show was so popular that it lasted on the air for over thirteen years, and eventually gained listeners throughout southeastern Michigan and Ohio. The program helped to publicize the various cultural, patriotic, and religious events, as well as the news concerning the Mexicans and Mexican Americans of Detroit and Michigan.

Gasca, Luis G.: A print-shop owner. He was the editor and publisher of *Prensa Libre* in 1930. The newspaper was known for its uncomplimentary comments regarding the Catholic Church. In 1932, he served as secretary of Liga de Obreros y Campesinos, an organization supported in part by Diego Rivera. During the repatriation of

Detroit's Mexican population, he returned to Mexico paying to have his printing press sent with him. He eventually became a successful printer in Mexico.

Guerrero, Jose: One of the first physicians serving the Spanish-speaking population of Detroit. His office was located on Woodward Avenue in Highland Park. He was a member of Circulo Mutualista.

Kern, Father Clement: The charismatic pastor of Holy Trinity Church from 1943 to 1977. He started his tenure at Holy Trinity Church as an assistant priest, before taking over the leadership of the church. He impressed the Mexican and Mexican American members of the church by learning how to read, write, and speak in Spanish, and by learning about their culture. Under his leadership the congregation grew, and he eventually established a large number of programs to assist the Spanish-speaking population of southeast Michigan.

Lopez, G. G.: A real estate agent, Lopez was a Spaniard involved in Detroit business beginning in 1919. He also assisted Detroit's Spanish-speaking population with legal problems and papers. His office was located at 3048 Bagley Avenue.

Lopez, Father J. C.: A priest who served a year at Holy Trinity Church. He arrived in 1939 in an effort to revitalize the church's congregation. At the church he founded Hijas de Mexico (Daughters of Mexico) and Caballeros de Cristo (Knights of Christ). Both organizations ceased to exist when he left the church in 1940 to work with *braceros* in the rural parts of Michigan.

Mendez, George: A lawyer from Mexico City. He came to Detroit in 1929. He was educated at Holy Trinity and St. Anne Schools. He graduated from Technical High School and from Wayne State University. He served as a speech instructor for several years, attending night school at Wayne State University's Law School. He was the first Mexican American admitted to the legal profession in southeastern Michigan. He was the first son of immigrant Mexicans to go to college and to enter a profession in Michigan's history. He handled the legal affairs for El Comite Patriotico Mexicano and the Mexican American Post #505 of the American Legion. He also served as legal consul for the Mexican Consulate's office in Detroit.

Mendoza, Samuel: Originally from Galveston, Texas. He was a graduate of the University of Texas. He came to Detroit in 1950. He practiced general medicine and had two offices in southwest Detroit.

Plata, George: First native Detroiter to become a lawyer. His father was a Mexican and his mother was German. He was a member of Circulo Mutualista. He attended Detroit Public Schools, eventually graduating from Western High School. He attended Wayne State University and Detroit College of Law. He served in World War II and in the Korean War as a Marine. He rose in rank from private to lieutenant, and then to captain as a reservist.

Pulido, Alberto: A real estate agent, Pulido came to Detroit in 1946 following World War II. His ancestors were from Nuevo Leon, Mexico. He attended night school at Wayne State University and worked for Burton Abstract Company and Industrial National Bank during the day. Starting in 1952, he operated a real estate agency at 24th Street and Bagley Avenue, and in 1958 he also worked for the Wayne County Road Commission. He served as commander of Mexican American Post #505 of the American Legion.

Vasquez, Ignacio: A renaissance man, Vasquez came to Detroit from Texas. He was considered by many to be the intellectual leader of Detroit's Mexican Colony. He was a teacher, journalist, artist, and poet. He worked as a translator in the export department of an automobile manufacturer. During the Depression, he made a living by teaching English and as the editor of a short-lived newspaper. He also painted murals in restaurants.

Mexican and Mexican American Celebrations

The celebrations listed below have been observed in Michigan since the arrival of the Mexican and Mexican American people in the state. Most of these celebrations are still observed by the Mexican and Mexican American population of Michigan today.

Cinco de Mayo (Fifth of May)

After Mexico gained its independence from Spain, England, Spain, and France loaned the newly formed country money to sustain it until it could stand on its own feet. In the years that followed England and Spain forgave the loan, but the French demanded repayment. When the Mexican government announced that the money would not be repaid until the country could afford to do so, the French invaded Mexico. In one of the initial battles, held on 5 May 1862, Mexican troops defeated the French at the Battle of Puebla. Although Mexico eventually fell to the French, this victory demonstrated Mexico's undying commitment to maintaining its freedom and identity. Cinco de Mayo honors the memory of those Mexicans that died in the battle, as well as the princi-ples that those Mexicans fought to protect.

El Día de los Muertos (The Day of the Dead)

El Día de los Muertos is celebrated on 2 November. On this day families visit the gravesites of loved ones. There they pay tribute to the individual in their own way. Some families clean the gravesite and place flowers, which are most often marigolds, the flower of the dead, on top of the grave. Some families paint the tombstone, or place mementos with special significance to the dearly departed somewhere near the gravesite or on top of the tombstone.

El Día de los Muertos is also a time when families erect an altar in their home dedicated to the spirits of those loved ones who have left this earth before them. Altars can be simple or elaborate. Altars, or *ofrendas,* as they are called, usually consist of objects that were used by or brought joy to the departed person's life. Among these objects are foods or drinks that were the person's favorite, as well as sculptures made of sugar that are known as "alfeniques." These objects may be sculpted as animals, miniature plates of food, small coffins, or skulls known as "calaveras." Often included with "ofrendas" is "papel picado," which literally translates to "little pieces of paper." On these pieces of paper, pictures relating to the theme of the Day of the Dead are cut out. The paper is then hung up around the altar. Completing the altar is a photograph of the person to whom the altar is dedicated, as well as items that serve as a testament to the person's accomplishments during his or her lifetime.

El Diez y Seis de Septiembre (The Sixteenth of September)

A celebration commemorating Mexico's independence from Spain. Specifically, this celebration commemorates the days of 15 and 16 September 1810. On the fifteenth, Father Miguel Hidalgo y Costilla sounded the bells of his village church in Dolores, Guanajuato, and then delivered the Grito de Dolores, a plea for Mexico's independence. This act gave birth to Mexico's fight for and eventual independence from Spain.

El Diez y Seis de Septiembre is often celebrated together by Mexicans and Mexican Americans living in a community. As part of the celebration, the famous cry of Father Hidalgo is reenacted on the

evening of the fifteenth, or on the following day. Celebrations in observance of El Diez y Seis de Septiembre differ from one community to the
next. In some communities folklorico dancers or bands perform, and
dealers sell their wares, goods, and foods in a marketplace. Games and
contests are also offered in carnival-like booths.

Fiestas Guadalupanas

Celebrations in observance of the Feast Day of La Virgen de Guadalupe,
the Virgen of Guadalupe, held on 12 December. The celebrations usually consist of a procession to the church led by a banner with a picture
of La Virgin de Guadalupe on it. After the celebratory mass a meal is
often held for all present. The meal is many times followed by a program celebrating Mexico's culture and heritage.

Las Posadas

The initial celebration of Christmas in Mexico took place in 1538 with
the arrival of Roman Catholic missionaries. As a component of that celebration, the story of Christ's birth, or *Nacimiento*, was observed, and
was called Las Posadas, which literally translates to "the inns." Las
Posadas commemorates the journey of Mary and Joseph into Bethlehem and their search for lodging. Las Posadas is traditionally observed
from 16 December to 24 December. The celebration includes traditional
songs and prayers, and often concludes with participants sharing some
refreshments or a meal, as well as children breaking a piñata.

At the heart of this celebration is a reenactment on Christmas Eve
of Mary and Joseph going through the streets of Bethlehem in search of
a place where Mary can rest. Reenactments can be as simple as Mary
and Joseph walking from room to room inside a house, where they are
turned away by "inn keepers," or as elaborate as Mary riding on a don-
key guided by Joseph through neighborhood streets. No matter the
venue, everyone present at the reenactment participates by singing the
verses *of Las Posadas,* which tells the story of Jesus' birth.

Traditional Mexican and Mexican American Foods

Flour Tortillas

3 cups all-purpose flour
¼ cup cold lard or hydrogenated shortening, cut into four pieces
½ tsp. salt
1 cup water

Place flour, shortening, and salt in a bowl. Mix the contents by hand until the consistency of cornmeal. Add water and mix until a ball forms.

Knead dough on a floured surface for 3 to 4 minutes. Cover and let rest for 10 minutes. Divide dough into ten balls of equal size. Roll out each ball to a circle an average of seven inches in diameter. Place the tortilla on a preheated, ungreased grill or frying pan. Turn the tortilla as it starts to form bubbles on top and repeat the process until browned on both sides. Adjust the heat to the cooking surface as needed.

Best when served hot off the stove. Can be saved if wrapped in aluminum foil, or placed inside a tortilla holder and refrigerated. To reheat use a microwave, a grill, or a stove's open flame turned down low. *Makes 10 tortillas.*

Frijoles

2 cups pinto, black, or red kidney beans

2 onions, finely chopped

2 cloves garlic, chopped

Sprig epazote or 1 bay leaf

2 or more Serrano chiles, chopped, or 1 tsp. dried pequin chiles, crumbled

3 Tbsp. lard or oil

Salt and pepper to taste

Rinse beans, but do not soak. Place beans in cold water to cover with half of the chopped onion and garlic, the epazote or bay leaf, and chiles. Cover and simmer gently, adding hot water as needed. Once beans start to wrinkle, add 1 tablespoon lard or oil. When beans soften, add seasonings. Cook another half hour without adding water. (The liquid will almost all be gone when the beans are done.)

Heat the remaining 2 tablespoons of lard or oil and sauté remaining chopped onion and garlic until limp. Let cook for 1 to 2 minutes. If needed, add a tablespoon of cooked beans and mash into the mixture. Add a second tablespoon of beans without draining them. This will allow some of the liquid created by the beans to evaporate.

Add a third tablespoon of beans and cook until a smooth, fairly heavy paste is formed. Return the contents to the bean pot and stir into beans over low heat to thicken the remaining liquid. *Makes 6–8 servings.*

Refried Beans

Cook beans as directed above. However, when mashing them, keep adding beans until all have been mashed into lard over low heat. From time to time add lard and cook until beans are creamy. A blender may be used to puree beans, in order to add them to the skillet bit by bit, and fry them dry in the hot lard. *Makes 6–8 servings.*

Arroz con Pollo (Rice with Chicken)

1 2½- to 3-pound boiler-fryer chicken, cut up

1 Tbsp. cooking oil

1½ cups long-grain rice

1 cup chopped onion

1 clove garlic, minced

3 cups water

1 7½-oz. can tomatoes, cut up

1 Tbsp. instant chicken bouillon granules

1 tsp. salt

¼ tsp. thread saffron, crushed

¼ tsp. pepper

1 cup frozen peas

1 2-oz. can sliced pimiento, drained and chopped

Sprinkle chicken lightly with salt. Brown chicken in hot oil in a 12-inch skillet. Remove chicken from skillet. In the pan drippings cook rice, onion, and garlic until rice is golden. Add water, tomatoes (undrained), bouillon granules, salt, saffron, and pepper. Bring contents to boiling point, making sure to stir the contents all the while. Place the chicken pieces on top of the rice mixture. Cover and allow to simmer for 30 to 35 minutes or until chicken is tender. Stir in peas and pimiento and then cover and cook for five additional minutes. *Makes 6 servings.*

Notes

1. Matt S. Meier and Feliciano Ribera, *Mexican Americans/American Mexicans* (New York: Hill and Wang, 1972), 111.

2. Zaragosa Vargas, *Proletarians of the North: A History of Mexican Industrial Workers in Detroit and the Midwest, 1917–1933* (Berkeley: University of California Press, 1993), 61.

3. Dennis Nodín Valdés, "Divergent Roots, Common Destinies? Latino Work and Settlement in Michigan," Julian Samora Research Institute, Michigan State University, Occasional Paper no. 4, May 1992.

4. Eduard Adam Skendzel, *Detroit's Pioneer Mexicans: A Historical Study of the Mexican Colony in Detroit* (Grand Rapids, Mich.: Littleshield Press, 1980), 16.

5. James L. Devlin, "Mexicans Hold Peace Service," *Detroit News,* 11 December 1920, 9.

6. Vargas, *Proletarians of the North,* 74.

7. James L. Devlin, "A Little Bit of Old Mexico Right Here in Detroit," *Detroit Sunday News,* 5 September 1920, 2.

8. Vargas, *Proletarians of the North,* 100–104.

9. *R. L. Polk's City Directory* (Detroit: R. L. Polk Company, 1918–29).

10. Marietta Lynn Baba and Malvina Hauk Abonyi, *Mexicans of Detroit* (Detroit: Center for Urban Studies, Wayne State University Press, 1979), 54–55.

11. Charles D. Cameron, "Our Spaniards and Aztecs," *Detroit Saturday Night*, 16 October 1926, 8.

12. Father Jose Alanis, *Annual Report of the Parish for 1923*, Archives of the Archdiocese of Detroit.

13. S. L. A. Marshall, "Mexican Labor Leaving Michigan for Homeland," *Detroit News*, 9 November 1932, 6.

14. Vargas, *Proletarians of the North*, 173.

15. S. L. A. Marshall, "Home Trek of Mexicans Marks End of an Epoch," *Detroit News*, 11 November 1932, 17.

16. Philip A. Adler, "69 Mexicans Say 'Adios,' Depart for Native Land," *Detroit News*, 10 October 1931, 4.

17. S. L. A. Marshall, "433 Bid Detroit Adios, Bound for Old Mexico," *Detroit News*, 16 November 1932, 4.

18. Ibid.

19. Marshall, "Home Trek," 17.

20. Skendzel, *Detroit's Pioneer Mexicans*, 17.

21. Ibid., 36.

22. David W. Hartman, ed., "Immigrants and Migrants: The Detroit Experience," *Journal of University Studies* 10 (fall 1974): 378–79.

23. Skendzel, *Detroit's Pioneer Mexicans*, 52.

24. E. Phillips Matz and Michael G. Roach, *The Story of Ste. Anne de Detroit Church, Michigan, 1701–1976, and the Bicentennial History of Catholic America* (Hackensack, N.J.: Custombook, 1976), 37.

25. Skendzel, *Detroit's Pioneer Mexicans*, 50.

26. Ibid., 54.

27. Hartman, "Immigrants and Migrants," 380.

28. Ibid., 387.

29. Chicano/Latino Studies Program, *Chicano/Latino Community Sourcebook* (East Lansing: Chicano/Latino Studies Program, Michigan State University, 1999), 13.

30. Lekan Oguntoyinbo, "More Hispanics Hold Office, but Barriers Hold up More Progress," *Detroit Free Press*, 1 October 1998, section B, 1–2.

31. Ibid., 2.

32. According to the U.S. Census of 2000, people of Hispanic ethnicity can include whites, blacks, and Asians who identify themselves as also being Hispanic.

33. Amber Arellano, "High Hopes for Future," *Detroit Free Press*, 29 March 2001, section B, 2.

34. Michigan House Democratic Caucus, "'Many Cultures, Many Faces' a Huge Success as Hispanics Gather at Capital to Celebrate," 9 October 2001, Press Release, *http://www.housedems.com/?CFID=260325&CFTOKEN=46506559*. Accessed 20 March 2002.

For Futher Reference

Aguilar, Louis. "Immigrants Collect U.S. Salaries while Retaining Cultural Ties." *Detroit Free Press*, 8 February 1999.

Baba, Marietta Lynn, and Malvina Hauk Abonyi. *Mexicans of Detroit*. (Detroit: Center for Urban Studies, Wayne State University Press, 1979).

Bodipo-Memba, Alejandro. "Death of a Dream: Why Detroit's Mexican Industries Failed." *Detroit Free Press*, 15 October 2001.

Cardenas, Edward L. "Hispanic influence keeps growing in Metro Detroit." *Detroit News*, 28 September 2000.

———. "Wounds Linger for Families of Deported Local Mexicans." *Detroit News*, 5 October 2000.

Cardenas, Reymundo. "The Mexican in Adrian." *Michigan History* 42 (1958).

Choldin, Harvey M., and Grafton M. Trout. *Mexican Americans in Transition: Migration and Employment in Michigan Cities*. (East Lansing: Rural Manpower Center and Department of Sociology, Michigan State University, 1969).

Cohen, Irwin. *Echoes of Detroit: A 300-Year History*. Haslett, Mich.: City Vision Publishing, 2000.

d'Eca, Raul, and A. Curtis Wilgus. *Latin American History*. (New York: Barnes & Noble Books, 1963).

Edson, George T. *Mexicans in Detroit, Michigan.* Paul S. Taylor Collection, Bancroft Library, University of California, Berkeley, 1926.

Esparza, Santiago. "Hispanics' Future Promising." *Detroit News,* 12 October 2000.

Garcia, Juan. "The People of Mexican Descent in Michigan: A Historical Overview." in *Blacks and Chicanos in Urban Michigan.* (Lansing: Michigan History Division, Michigan Department of State, 1979).

Humphrey, Norman Daymond. "Mexican Repatriation from Michigan: Public Assistance in Historical Perspective" in *Social Science Review* 15 (1941).

———. "The Migration and Settlement of Detroit Mexicans" in *Economic Geography* 19 (1943).

———. "Employment Patterns of Mexicans in Detroit" in *Monthly Labor Review* 61 (1945).

Kozlowski, Kim. "Mexicans Embrace Southwest Detroit." *Detroit News,* 21 December 2000.

McWilliams, Carey. *North from Mexico: The Spanish-Speaking People of the United States.* (Westport, Conn.: Greenwood Press, 1968).

Meier, Matt S., and Feliciano Ribera. *Mexican Americans/American Mexicans.* (New York: Hill and Wang, 1972).

R. L. Polk's City Directory. Detroit: R. L. Polk Company, 1918–29.

Skendzel, Eduard Adam *Detroit's Pioneer Mexicans: A Historical Study of the Mexican Colony in Detroit.* (Grand Rapids, Mich.: Littleshield Press, 1980).

Slaughter, Jane. "Mexican Industries Closes Detroit Plants, Making Good on 1999 Threat." in *Labor Notes,* August 2001.

Valdés, Dennis Nodín. *El Pueblo Mexicano en Detroit y Michigan.* (Detroit: Wayne State University Press, 1982).

———. *Materials on the History of Latinos in Michigan and the Midwest: An Annotated Bibliography.* (Detroit: College of Education, Wayne State University, 1982).

———. *Al Norte: Agricultural Workers in the Great Lakes Region, 1917–1970.* (Austin: University of Texas Press, 1991).

———. "Divergent Roots, Common Destinies? Latino Work and Settlement in Michigan." Julian Samora Research Institute, Michigan State University, Occasional Paper no. 4, May 1992.

Vargas, Zaragosa. *Proletarians of the North: A History of Mexican Industrial*

Workers in Detroit and the Midwest, 1917–1933. (Berkeley: University of California Press, 1993).

Wilson, Kay Diekman. "The Historical Development of Migrant Labor in Michigan Agriculture." M.A. thesis, Michigan State University, 1977.

Wolfe, Bertram D. *The Fabulous Life of Diego Rivera.* (New York: Stein and Day, 1963).

Index